ROME
UP CLOSE

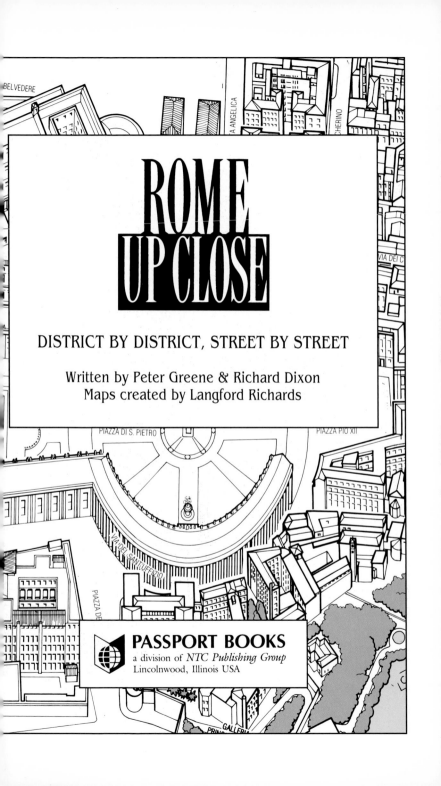

ROME UP CLOSE

DISTRICT BY DISTRICT, STREET BY STREET

Written by Peter Greene & Richard Dixon
Maps created by Langford Richards

PASSPORT BOOKS
a division of *NTC Publishing Group*
Lincolnwood, Illinois USA

This edition published 1995 by Passport Books,
Trade Imprint of NTC Publishing Group, 4255 West Touhy Avenue,
Lincolnwood (Chicago), Illinois 60646-1975 U.S.A.

Conceived, edited and designed by
Duncan Petersen Publishing Ltd,
31, Ceylon Road,
London W14 OYP

Originated by Reprocolor International, Milan, Italy
Printed by GraphyCems, Navarra, Spain
*Cover photo:*Ted Lacey

Every reasonable care has been taken to ensure the information in
this guide is accurate, but the publishers and copyright holders can
accept no responsibility for the consequences of errors in the text or
on the maps, especially those arising from closures, or those topo-
graphical changes ocurring after completion of the aerial survey on
which the maps are based.

Library of Congress Catalog Card Number:94-77723

ACKNOWLEDGEMENTS

The authors would like to thank the following people for their invaluable help and advice: Paola Bartoccini and Roberta Battagli; Claudia Galli; Laura Marino and Daniela Martellucci of the Rome EPT; Italo Grilli; and SPQR- *Senatus Populusque Romanus* to whom this book is dedicated.

Editorial

Editorial director	Andrew Duncan
Assistant editor	Joshua Dubin

Design

Art director	Mel Petersen
Designers	Chris Foley and Beverley Stewart
Aerial survey by	Kamera Studio
Maps created by	Langford Richards

Contents

The indexes are essential features of these guides. In particular, **the index of points of interest** provides, under convenient and obvious headings such as shops, museums, cafés, bars and restaurants, a quick-reference listing of essential practical and sightseeing information: instant access to the guide and to the city.

About this book

How the mapping was made

Isometric mapping is produced from aerial photographic surveys. For this book, aerial photography was provided by Kamera Studio Rome.

Scores of enlargements were made from the negatives, which Langford and Richards then used to complete the task.

Isometric projection means that verticals are the same height, whether in the foreground or in the background – at the 'front' (bottom) of the page or at the 'back' (top). Thus the diminishing effect of perspective is avoided and all the buildings, whether near or distant, are shown in similar detail and appear at an appropriate height.

The order of the maps

The map squares are arranged in sequence running from north to south and from west to east. For further details, see the master location map on page 24–25.

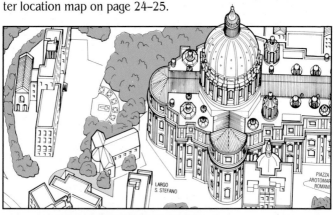

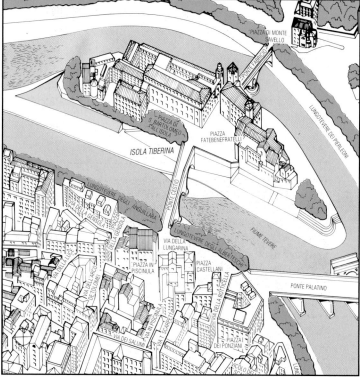

Numerals on maps

Each numeral on a map cross refers to the text printed on the facing page. The numbers generally read from the top left of each map to the bottom right, in a west-east direction. However, there are deviations from this pattern when several interesting features occur together, or within one street.

Opening and closing times Unless indicated otherwise in the text, opening times generally follow these rules: most museums are open from 9am to 1.30pm while art galleries close at 2pm. With the important exception of the Vatican Museums and Castel Sant'Angelo, they are closed on Mondays. Although a few also have occasional afternoon opening hours, it is wise to limit visits to the morning. The main archaeological sites close around 3pm in winter and 6pm or 7pm in summer. Churches, apart from the main basilicas which are open all day, are more fickle but generally open from 8am to 12.30pm and from 5pm to 7.30pm. One of the city's less endearing habits is the lengthy closure of sights for *restauro* (often a euphemism for shortages of staff or funds or both). In this event, do as the Romans: just be thankful when you find something open.

Prices Restaurants

L   means one person can eat for less than 30,000 lire.

LL   means one person can eat for 30-60,000 lire.

LLL   means one person generally pays more than 60,000 lire.

Hotels

L   means a double room is less than 150,000 lire per night.

LL   means a double room is 150-250,000 lire per night.

LLL   means a double room is more than 250,000 lire per night.

Out of season, hotels often offer considerably lower prices.

Dates

BC dates are given in the usual way, with BC after the date. The prefix AD has been used only for dates up to and including AD 100; thereafter, no AD prefix is used.

The terms **trecento, quattrocento, cinquecento** and **seicento** are generally used in connection with Italian art or architecture of the thirteen, fourteen, fifteen and sixteen hundreds.

Coverage Rome – its language, its laws, its architecture and its religion have hardly left any corner of the world untouched. Still today it weaves an irresistible spell on the visitor, but its charm is in its details, not just the celebrated tourist set-pieces. This guide provides the ideal key to just such details. The writers, building on the unique nature of the mapping, have concentrated on the rich variety of Rome rather than simply the obvious and well-known sights. For the first-time visitor, however, Rome in a Nutshell (pages 12-13) lists the city's unmissable attractions. Much historical background, essential to an understanding of Rome's evolution, has been included along with plenty of practical information on such things as eating and shopping. Ever since the publication in the 12thC of *Mirabilia Urbis Romae*, grandfather of modern guide books, accounts of Rome have inextricably mixed legend with fact to such an extent that the colourful stories have become as much a part of the city as its very stones; here, too, we hope that this guide will not disappoint.

Rome in a nutshell:
the sights you should not miss

THE ETERNAL CITY cannot be seen in a day. More than 2,700 years of history have left it overloaded with outstanding sights. These two pages give a list of the essential things to see, together with the page numbers of the maps on which they appear – even the most hurried visitor should not miss them.

This guide, however, is not just an introduction to Rome's star turns; it is also a way to discover the less celebrated features of the world's most historically interesting city. In the days of the 18thC Grand Tour, aristocratic visitors hired the services of a personal *cicerone*, or erudite local guide: this guide is your modern equivalent.

The essential city:

The relics of Classical Rome scatter the city. The best preserved of all is the **Pantheon** (page 74). The most extensive ruins lie to the south of Piazza Venezia. The **Colosseum** (page 122) is the grandest survivor; nearby, the **Roman Forum** (pages 100 & 102) is still haunted by the ghosts of the ancient city while **Trajan's Column** (page 78) brilliantly records Rome's military triumphs.

St Peter's (page 40), the world's largest church, is the lode star for Catholic Rome while the basilicas of **St John Lateran** (page 124) and **Santa Maria Maggiore** (page 86) have an architectural harmony that their big sister somehow lacks. The highlights among the city's smaller churches include **Santa Prassede** with its glowing mosaics (page 86) and Bernini's Baroque pearl, **Sant'Andrea al Quirinale** (page 58).

Along with Michelangelo's frescoes for the **Sistine Chapel** (page 40, part of Vatican Museums), obligatory stops for art lovers are the churches of **San Luigi dei Francesi** (page 72) and **Santa Maria del Popolo** (page 26) for their masterpieces by Caravaggio, and **Santa Maria della Vittoria** (page 62) for Bernini's sculpture of St Teresa.

The **Vatican Museums** (page 40) are the world's greatest treasure house, while the **Capitoline Museums** (page 98), the world's oldest public collection, have an incomparable hoard of Classical sculpture.

To feel the pulse of Roman life, head for one of Rome's magnificent squares, each with its fountain. **Piazza di Spagna** and the **Spanish Steps** (page 32) provide a romantic Baroque backdrop to the city's traditional tourist meeting place; in the market square of **Campo de' Fiori** (page 92) you can watch Roman daily life at its most animated. The **Trevi Fountain** (page 56) and Bernini's **Four Rivers** in Piazza Navona (page 72) vie for the title of Rome's finest fountain.

The medieval warren of **Trastevere** (pages 110-114), – across the Tiber – is the place for restaurants and nightlife, although it is becoming just a little too popular. Those in the know eat in the **Ghetto** (Page 94). **Via Condotti** (Page 32) and its neighbours are the most elegant of Rome's shopping streets.

For unforgettable **views**, climb up to the **Pincio** (Page 26) to see the sunset behind the dome of St Peter's or look out at the Colosseum from up on the **Palatine Hill** (page 120).

VISITOR INFORMATION

Transport

From airports to city

Leonardo da Vinci Airport at Fiumicino, some 30 km to the south-west of the city, is Rome's principal international touchdown. An hourly train service between 7.25 am and 10.25 pm (journey time 30 minutes, cost 12,000 lire) runs to Rome's main Termini railway station.

An ACOTRAL bus service provides an hourly night-time service between the airport and Piazzale dei Partigiani near Stazione Termini. The official yellow taxis charge a supplement of 10,000 lire on trips from the airport. Together with the fare on the meter, a journey downtown should amount to around 60,000 lire.

Ciampino Airport, some 16 km to the south-east, mostly serves charter flights; the best transport link is by ACOTRAL bus to Anagnina station at the end of the Metropolitana Line A from where a 25-minute journey takes you to the centre. The equivalent taxi ride will cost around 50,000 lire. You are well advised to ignore the numerous taxi and hotel touts at both airports.

City orientation All roads in Rome eventually lead to the foot of the wedding cake mass of the Monumento Nazionale whose bulk looms up when you least expect it. Although it may spoil the view, it is a useful place to take your bearings. From it, Via del Corso runs northwards to Piazza del Popolo and the gateway to the Via Flaminia, Rome's historic route to Northern Europe; to the west, Corso Vittorio Emanuele II heads for the Tiber and the threshold of the Vatican City, while to the east Via Nazionale bull-dozes its way to the Piazza della Repubblica and Termini Station.

Don't imagine that you will find the delights of Rome in these main streets. Head off, rather, into the narrow backstreets – the narrower the better – to discover the true magic. Historic Rome is compact and best explored on foot – a not-too-hurried stroll will take you from Termini Station to St Peter's in less than an hour.

Streets, although clearly marked, frequently follow a disorientating system of numbering – they are numbered consecutively up one side and then back down the other.

Buses In a city centre made for walking, only a few of the comprehensive orange ATAC bus routes will be of interest to tourists. The ATAC information office in Piazza dei Cinquecento in front of Stazione Termini can provide you with a colourful, if complicat-

> **Tufa and travertine**
> You will find these terms used throughout the guide. They refer to two types of stone.
>
> Much of early Rome was built from the soft, easily carved volcanic rock known as tufa. However, as Roman building skills developed, a white to pale grey limestone known as travertine became the dominant building material. The facing of the Colosseum is the finest example of its use, but you will see it everywhere. More than any other, it is Rome's distinctive stone.

ed, route map. The electric minibus service, Linea 119, meanders through much of the medieval *centro storico*, while the popular tourist Linea 64 links the Vatican with Termini Station by way of Piazza Venezia (beware of pick-pockets on this route).

Cheap, flat-fare tickets for all urban routes can be bought from tobacconists and news vendors; cancel them in the machine at the back of the bus on boarding – you then have an hour and a half to complete your journey.

ATAC also runs Linea 110, a three-hour tourist round trip which takes in Rome's most celebrated sights. It leaves daily at 3.30 pm from Piazza dei Cinquecento (in winter Sat only at 2.30 pm) and the 6,000-lire ticket must be bought beforehand from the information office on the square.

Metro Although limited to two lines, Rome's modern subway system, La Metropolitana – La Metro for short – usefully links a number of important tourist haunts. Linea A runs from Ottaviano, near the Vatican Museums, to the southern suburbs beyond Cinecittà taking in Piazza di Spagna, Piazza della Repubblica and Stazione Termini. Linea B goes from Rebibbia in the north-east by way of Termini Station to the futuristic suburb of EUR taking in Via Cavour, the Colosseum and Circo Massimo. As for buses, flat-fare tickets for La Metro are sold at tobacconists and newsagents as well as at stations. A one-day pass, the BIG, allows unlimited travel on buses and Metro and costs 2,800 lire.

Taxis Fares in Rome's yellow taxis are reasonable and special lanes ensure they don't get too snarled up in the traffic. The meter starts at 6,400 lire (with supplements for baggage, night and Sunday services). They can be picked up at the stands in most major piazzas or cruising along the main streets. Drivers expect a tip of around 10 per cent.

Private cars Rome's chaotic traffic is nothing new; some 2,000 years ago Juvenal was already complaining about it. Roman driving is in a class of its own and few visitors would be wise to test their nerve against the natives'. Besides, much of the historic centre is now closed to all but permit holders, parking is a nightmare, and figures for car theft are appallingly high. If you are brave, or foolhardy enough to bring your car to Rome, the emergency breakdown number for the Italian Automobile Club, ACI, is 116, and virtually the only secure public central garage parking is under the Villa Borghese gardens.

Useful data
Tourist information For information before you go, the Italian State Tourist Board (ENIT) has offices in most important capital cities. In Rome, the three offices of the Rome Provincial Tourist Board (EPT) have a wealth of advice on accommodation, trans-

---

Republican and Imperial Rome: a potted history
The earliest days of Rome are lost in legend. Tradition claims that it was founded by Romulus in 753 BC and was ruled over for some two hundred years as a growing city state by a succession of seven kings. Following the expulsion of the last of these kings, Tarquin the Proud, the great period of the Roman Republic started in 509 BC. It lasted for almost five hundred years and witnessed the consolidation of Rome's conquests and its rise to unprecedented power. Cracks began to appear in the Republic during the 1stC BC; when Julius Caesar crossed the Rubicon river and seized power in 49 BC the Republic was finished in all but name. In 27 BC Octavian, taking the name Augustus, became the first Roman emperor, ushering in the era of Imperial Rome. It was a time of grandiose building projects and much of the Ancient Rome still visible today dates from the Imperial period.

The later days of Imperial Rome were marked by ever more damaging attacks by barbarian hordes from the north. Finally, in AD 476, Odoacer, King of the Goths, threw out the last of the Roman emperors and became King of Italy.

---

port, museums and shopping, and multi-lingual staff. You will find them at:
– The customs area of Leonardo da Vinci Airport at Fiumicino (tel. 6011255); open 8.15 am to 7 pm, Mon-Sat.
– Stazione Termini near platform 6 (tel. 4871270); open as above and Sun.
– 5, Via Parigi, near Piazza della Repubblica (tel.4883748); open as Airport.

Visitors to the Vatican can get help from the Vatican Information Office on St Peter's Square (tel. 6984466); open 8.30 am to 7 pm Mon-Sat, 8 am to 2 pm Sun.

Sightseeing tours The ATAC tourist bus 110 (see page 15) is the cheapest way to get your bearings on first arriving in Rome. The Rome Tourist Board can give you details of a number of reputable companies who offer inexpensive guided coach tours, including:
– American Express, 38 Piazza di Spagna (tel. 67641).
– CIT, 68 Piazza della Repubblica (tel. 47941).

Private guided tours For the services of an authorized tourist guide, contact CISL Tourist Guide office, 12 Rampa Mignanelli below the Spanish Steps (tel. 6789842).

Trotting tours A romantic, if expensive, way of seeing the sights is in one of Rome's celebrated *carrozzelle*, or horse-drawn carriages. A one-hour trot for up to five people will leave little change from a 100,000 lire note. Always negotiate the price before starting. Stands are at St Peter's Square, Piazza di Spagna, the Colosseum, Piazza Venezia, Piazza Navona, the Trevi Fountain and Via Veneto.

Shopping, banking and business hours
Most shops open around 9 am and lock up between 7 and 8 pm but close for a lengthy lunch from 1 pm to 4 or 5 pm. Shutters are firmly up on Sundays. Most food stores close on Thursday afternoons while other shops close on Monday mornings. In the summer months, many shops also close on Saturday afternoons. In August, when the city becomes a ghost town, much of Rome closes up.

Banks are open from 8.30 am to 1.30 pm and 2.45 pm to 3.45 pm Mon-Fri only. Most of them offer foreign exchange services (*cambio*) but rates can vary, so shop around if changing large amounts. Exchange bureaux in tourist centres have similiar hours

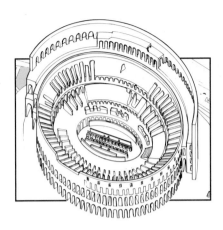

to shops, but offer poorer rates, while cashing travellers cheques in hotels usually gives the worst rate of all. If you are caught short, the bigger central banks are currently introducing out-of-hours automatic exchange machines which take bank notes of most major currencies; convenient ones can be found at 43, Piazza Barberini, and 399, Via del Corso.

State and local government offices open early in the morning and are all firmly closed by 2 pm, although plans are afoot to bring them into line with standard European business hours. Private concerns, however, follow the usual 9 to 5 routine.

Public holidays
New Year's Day; 6 Jan (La Befana); Easter Monday; 25 April (Liberation Day); 1 May; 29 June (Rome's patron saints, Sts Peter and Paul); 15 August (Assumption); 1 Nov (All Saints'); 8 Dec (Immaculate Conception); Christmas Day; 26 Dec (Santo Stefano).

Postal services
Stamps are easily purchased from any tobacconist – look out for the T sign. Rome's central Post Office in Piazza San Silvestro is open from 8.30 am to 9 pm Mon-Fri, 8.30 am to noon Sat and has a *post restante* service (letters should be addressed to Fermo Posta, Posta Centrale, Piazza San Silvestro, 00186). Italy's postal service is notoriously slow and your postcards have a better chance of reaching home before you do if they are sent by the Vatican post – the stamps are also much more colourful (The Vat-

ican Post Office is in St Peter's Square).

Telephones

Standard payphones, found both on main streets and in many bars, take 100, 200 and 500 lire coins as well as *gettoni*, the special 200 lire telephone tokens often used as small change. Many also take phone cards, available in units of 5,000 and 10,000 lire from newspaper kiosks and tobacconists – a more convenient way to make long distance calls. Calls from your hotel will cost appreciably more than from standard payphones. All telephone numbers in the text presume you are calling from within the city; for calls from outside Rome add the prefix 06 (from abroad just 6). To make international direct-dialled calls use 00 + your country code.

Some useful numbers

– For help from the operator for calls within Italy dial 10.
– For information on international calls, dial 176 for Europe and Mediterranean countries, 1790 for non-European countries; to make operator-assisted international calls dial 15 for the former and 170 for the latter.
– In dire emergencies dial police, fire and ambulances on 113 (no charge).
– For *l'ora esatta*, the speaking clock, dial 161.
– For the Questura Centrale, Rome's main police station, call 4686.

Publications

The Rome Tourist Board (see tourist information, page 16) publishes the monthly *Carnet di Roma* which lists forthcoming events in Italian, English, French and German. The daily newspaper *La Repubblica* produces a Thursday magazine supplement to its Rome edition called *Trovaroma* which lists, in Italian naturally, the events of the week as well as restaurants and nightclubs.

The travel sections of large bookshops (Libreria Feltrinelli at 84, Via V.E. Orlando near Piazza della Repubblica, is a good choice) hold a comprehensive range of guides to Rome in both Italian and foreign languages. The Economy Book Center at 136 Via Torino and the Lion Bookshop in Via della Fontanella specialize in English language books; Herder at 117 Piazza Montecitorio is Rome's German bookseller. There is also the Libreria Francese at 23 Piazza San Luigi de' Francesi and the Libreria

Spagnola at 90 Piazza Navona.

Foreign Embassies

- **Australia** 215 Via Alessandria; tel. 832721.
- **Austria** 3 Via Pergolesi; tel. 868241.
- **Belgium** 49 Via Monti Parioli; tel. 3224441.
- **Canada** 27 Via GB de Rossi; tel. 8415341.
- **France** 87 Piazza Farnese; tel. 686011.
- **Germany** 25 Via Po; tel. 8441812.
- **Great Britain** 80A Via XX Settembre; tel. 4825651.
- **Ireland** 3 Large del Nazareno; tel. 6782541.
- **Netherlands** 8 Via Mercati; tel.3221141.
- **New Zealand** 28 Via Zara; tel. 4402928.
- **Spain** 19 Largo Fontanella Borghese; tel. 6878264.
- **USA** 119 Via Vittorio Veneto; tel. 46741.

Medical information

European Community residents are entitled to treatment under reciprocal arrangements provided that they carry the necessary documentation (Form E111). Other nationals are well advised to take out private travel insurance which will indemnify them – provided they have proper receipts for any treatment.

Hospital

Apart from emergency services obtainable by telephoning 113, ambulances can be called from the Italian Red Cross on 5100. The following central hospitals have a 24-hour *pronto soccorso*, or casualty department:
- Ospedale di Fatebenefratelli, Isola Tiberina; tel.58731.
- Policlinico Umberto I, Viale del Policlinico; tel.49971.
- Ospedale San Giacomo, 29 Via Canova; tel.67261.
- Santo Spirito, Lungotevere in Sassia; tel. 6838901.

Late-night pharmacies

Central Roman chemists which stay open throughout the night include: Farmacia della Stazione at 24 Piazza dei Cinquecento (tel. 4880019); Internazionale at 49 Piazza Barberini (tel. 4871195); and Spinedi at 73 Via Arenula (tel. 6543278). Information on other late-night pharmacies is available by telephoning 1921.

Doctors

For minor ailments, pharmacists are often able to help without reference to a doctor. The *Pagine Gialle*, Rome's Yellow Pages, has a list of doctors under *Medici*, although it is easier to seek recommendations from your hotel porter. A night-time service is available through the *Guardia Medica* on 4756741-4.

Dental treatment
The standard of dentistry in Italy is generally very high, but it is also expensive. Again, the Yellow Pages list dentists, though rec-ommendation from your hotel porter is probably a more reliable course.

Safety
Petty theft is as rife in Rome as in any other Western capital but common sense should keep you out of trouble. Look out for the innocent-looking street urchins who hang around the main tourist haunts – while one thrusts a card under your nose asking for money, the others rifle your pockets. Don't carry large amounts of money and hold on tight to wallets or handbags. Photocopies of documents kept in your room are invaluable if you are unlucky enough to lose the originals. Thefts should be reported to the Questura Centrale, 15 Via San Vitale.

Beyond the city centre
First-time visitors will be hard pressed to see a tenth of what the city centre has to offer. However, a number of Rome's outlying monuments merit attention and lie within easy reach.

• **Baths of Caracalla**, south of the Colosseum, Metro Linea B to Circo Massimo. The ruins of Caracalla's great *thermae*, built 212-7, are remarkably intact. The titanic brick walls which still rise above the umbrella pines give an idea of their grandeur, though the marble cladding and statues have long gone. While only half the size of Diocletian's Baths – holding a mere 1,600 bathers – these were the most luxurious public baths in the Empire and remained in use until the Goths cut the water supply in the 6thC.

• **The Appian Way**, south of the city; bus 118 from Colosseum. Via Appia Antica, the original Roman Appian Way, was the earliest of Rome's great roads, built in 312 BC. The first stretch beyond the city walls, still paved with huge basalt cobbles, seems to have altered little over the centuries. Early Christians met in secret along this road and have left some of the world's most extraordi-nary cemeteries – the catacombs; that of St Calixtus is the largest, tunnelled out on four underground levels over a period of 300 years and covering a total area of more than 100,000 square metres.

• **Hadrian's Villa**, train to Tivoli from Stazione Termini. Some 35 km east of Rome, Hadrian built the largest and most sybaritic villa in the Roman Empire. The substantial ruins and beautiful gardens are haunted by the ghost of one of Rome's most enlightened emperors.

• **Ostia Antica**, train from Termini Metro Linea B, change at Magliana. The ruins of the port of ancient Rome, now marooned inland, stretch over a vast area and have been remarkably well preserved by the sands that covered them. Perhaps only at Pompeii can you find another Roman town as complete as this.

Beyond Rome By train The Italian state railways are cheap and prompt. All inter-city trains leave from Stazione Termini (apart from a limited service from Stazione Ostiense). Destinations served by direct trains include Florence, Milan, Bologna and Naples. Automatic machines at the information office at Stazione Termini (tel. 47751) save you a long wait at the desks.

By bus Rome has no long-distance bus station and, although cheap, travel by coach is complicated by the lack of clear information – each region is served by its own private bus service. Most leave from Viale L Einaudi to the north of Piazza dei Cinquecento with destinations shown on signs in the windscreens.

By air Although expensive, domestic flights in Italy are useful for reaching the peninsula's more distant cities. Alitalia has a comprehensive service from both Fiumicino and Ciampino. The central Rome office is at 13 Via Bissolati (information tel. 5456).

By car Car hire in Italy is expensive – you will get a better deal with a Fly-Drive package from your travel agent. Car rental firms have offices at both airports; for city-centre offices check in Rome's *Pagine Gialle*, or Yellow Pages. Few firms rent to anyone under 21 and a stiff deposit is usually demanded. All documents must be with you in the car at all times.

THE
ISOMETRIC
MAPS

Master location map

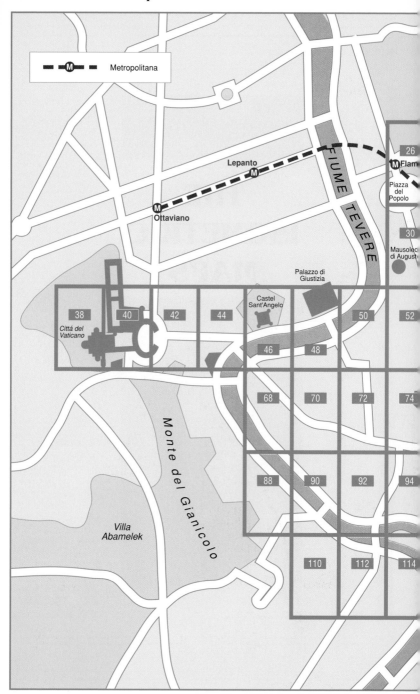

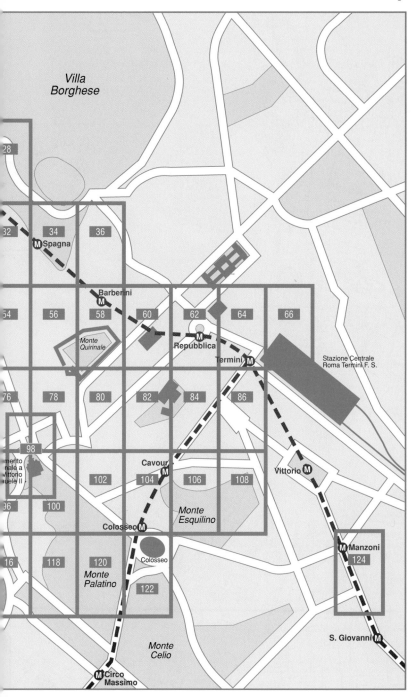

VIA FLAMINIA

VIALE G. WASHINGTON

VIALE DEL MURO TORTO

①

② PIAZZALE FLAMINIO

③

④

PIAZZA DEL POPOLO

⑤

⑥ PIAZZALE NAPOLEONE I

VIALE DEL BELVEDERE

VIALE G. D'ANNUNZIO

PIAZZA DEL POPOLO

⑦

VIA DELL'OCA

VIA DI RIPETTA

⑧

⑨

⑩

⑪

⑫

⑬

⑭

⑮

⑯

⑰

VIA DEL CORSO

VIA A. BRUNETTI

VIA DELLE FONTANELLA

VIA DEL BABUINO

VIA MARGUTTA

VIA MARGUTTA

VICOLO DEL BABUINO

Since the days of Republican Rome this has been the main gateway to the city – few places can boast such a striking entrance.① The ancient **Via Flaminia**, built in 220 BC, starts its long journey across Italy from ② **Piazzale Flaminio**, a tangle of traffic on the improvised ring road that circles central Rome. ③ The 16thC **Porta del Popolo** provides a monumental gateway to Valadier's striking **Piazza del Popolo**. Huddling beside it is ④ the chaste, early Renaissance façade of **Santa Maria del Popolo**. The church was built on an 11thC chapel erected to exorcise the malign spirit of Nero; his ashes were reputedly buried hereabouts. Inside are art treasures that alone would warrant a visit to Rome – Caravaggio's horribly palpable rendering of the Crucifixion of St Peter together with his Conversion of St Paul and Raphael's sublime Chigi chapel. At the centre of the sweeping square, ⑤ the 3,000- year-old **obelisk**, which Augustus brought from Heliopolis to decorate the Circus Maximus, was placed here a mere 400 years ago. To the east of the square rise the tree-clad flanks of the **Pincio**. At the summit of its shaded steps is the famous sunset view of the city from ⑥ the **Belvedere** in Piazzale Napoleone I. From a table outside ⑦ **Rosati** you can admire the square at its best – be prepared to pay for the privilege. ⑧ **Santa Maria dei Miracoli** and ⑨ **Santa Maria in Montesanto** seem like twin churches, but look carefully to see how Rainaldi's Baroque trickery makes two differently shaped buildings appear the same. They mark the start of a trident of three great streets. ⑩ To the west, **Via di Ripetta** sets a course for the Vatican; ⑪ Roman food with a touch of fantasy at **Porto di Ripetta** (LLL) while across the road **Cose Fritte** sells civilized Rome's answer to fast food – deep-fried battered salt cod, vegetables and take-away *pizza al taglio* (L). ⑫ **Via del Corso** in the centre runs straight as a die to the Forum. Tucked away in Via della Fontanella, ⑬ **Hotel Valadier** offers high-tech luxury (LLL). Opposite is one of Rome's best English-language booksellers, ⑭ the **Lion Bookshop**. To the east, ⑮ **Via del Babuino** marches south to Piazza di Spagna; ⑯ **Cesari** at No. 15 has ritzy furnishing fabrics – above the patrician main sales floor it also sells *scampoli*, masses of remnants at prices more suited to the plebian purse. There is an imaginative vegetarian menu in the cool, bohemian atmosphere of ⑰ I Margutta, (119, Via Margutta) – relatively inexpensive (L).

▼ 32

Back in the 1stC AD, the Roman Epicurean Lucullus built his gardens on the Pincio; so too did the Pinci family who left their name to the hill. The modern-day park was laid out by Valadier in the 1810s with wide, bust-lined promenades shaded by tall planes, pines and evergreen oaks. The works of ① the bucolic **water clock**, built by a 19thC Dominican monk, look terminally gummed up, but still it stands as one of the city's more eccentric fountains. ② The **obelisk** is a Roman copy, one of the many monuments that a grieving Emperor Hadrian erected to his drowned favourite, Antinous. ③ A **foot bridge** spans Viale del Muro Torto linking the Pincio with Villa Borghese; down below, the road skirts the crooked section of the ancient Aurelian wall, the Muro Torto, said to be under the protection of St Peter and thus never breached. Jacob More, a Scottish painter, cast ④ the **gardens of Villa Borghese** in the English Style in 1773. Rome's largest public park makes a fitting back-drop for the Borghese Gallery (off map), housing Cardinal Scipione Borghese's 17thC collection of sculpture and painting that vies in quality with the museums of the Vatican. The weathered, neo-Classical cube of ⑤ Valadier's **Casina** is now a restaurant – its outstanding setting counts rather more than the food (LLL). Nearby, ⑥ a **bust** to the Italian astronomer Angelo Secchi has a hole in the base to mark the point where Rome's very own meridian passes. ⑦ Through the railings above a low wall you can catch a glimpse of the clipped avenues of the gardens of the **Villa Medici** (see page 33). ⑧ The melodramatic 19thC **monument to the Cairoli brothers**, a pair of Garibaldian heroes who fell trying to enter Rome in 1867, bears more than a passing resemblance to a Wild West shoot-out.

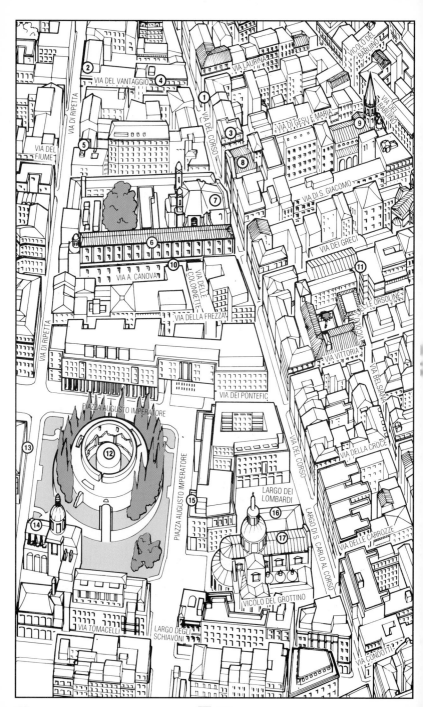

The Corso to the Mausoleum of Augustus

Horse races, or *corse*, run along this former stretch of the Roman Via Flaminia, lent their name to ① **Via del Corso**. Banned at the end of the 19thC, they provided a furious finale to the Roman Carnival. Above the undistinguished shops stand noble palaces. ② **Enoteca Buccone** (19, Via Ripetta) is a cornucopia of Italy's best wines. ③ Goethe fell in love with Rome while staying at **20, Via del Corso**. Horses with a handicap, or *vantaggio*, galloped off from ④ *Via del Vantaggio*. The advantage at ⑤ **La Buca di Ripetta** (36, Via di Ripetta) is outstanding Roman cooking at fair prices (LL). ⑥ The medieval **hospital of San Giacomo in Augusta** succoured pilgrims arriving in Rome along the Via Flaminia; remedies for incurable syphilis were the speciality, hence the adjoining church, ⑦ **San Giacomo degli Incurabili**. The Bolognetti family put on a lively sideshow above their tombs in ⑧ Rainaldi's lavish High Baroque church of **Gesù e Maria**. ⑨ The neo-Gothic Anglican **Church of All Saints**, a legacy of Rome's 19thC English ghetto, sits demurely in Via Babuino. In **Via Antonio Canova**, ⑩ the studio of the celebrated sculptor is encrusted with a jig-saw puzzle of antique fragments. ⑪ A former monastery now houses Rome's premier music academy, the **Conservatorio di Musica Santa Cecilia**. ⑫ The **Mausoleum of Augustus**, the massive cylindrical tomb of Rome's first Emperor (started 29 BC) was later used as a medieval fortress, stone quarry, garden, amphitheatre and, finally, a concert hall with famed acoustics. Mussolini, lest anyone should forget that he was the new Augustus, cleared the whole area leaving the mausoleum in stately solitude; the building now stands abandoned and surrounded by glum Fascist architecture (the *palazzo* to the north bears the date XIX – Year 19 in the Fascist calendar). Between the mausoleum and the Tiber, ⑬ the **Ara Pacis Augustae** (off map), the Altar of Augustan Peace, was re-erected here in the 1930s in a huge glass case. Featuring some of the most beautiful Roman relief carving yet found, this altar was built around 10 BC to celebrate the arrival of peace under the rule of Augustus. On the right hand side of ⑭ the fresh-faced Baroque church of **San Rocco**, a stone pilaster set in the wall marks Tiber flood levels since the 16thC. ⑮ Legendary *fettuccine* at **Alfredo al Augusteo** (LL) while ⑯ **La Capricciosa** (L) claims to have invented the eponymous pizza. Pietro da Cortona's vast dome (1668) atop ⑰ **San Carlo al Corso** is one of the city's landmarks.

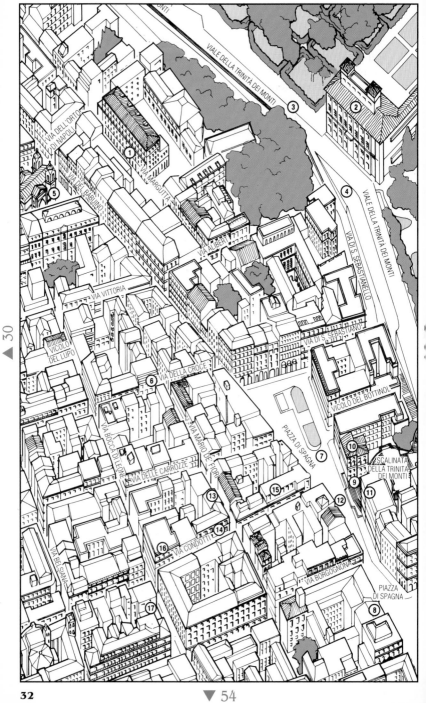

Piazza di Spagna, once the haunt of English milords on the Grand Tour, is still a magnet for foreign visitors. ① In **Via Margutta** antiquarian shops are stifling the bohemian atmosphere of this artists' quarter. ② The solid bastion of the 16thC **Villa Medici** presents an impregnable face; ③ a nearby **column** records Galileo's house arrest in the villa. ④ Green oasis and good coffee at **Ciampini al Café du Jardin**. Via del Babuino gets its name from ⑤ the mangy **statue of Silenus**, dubbed a baboon by locals. Along with elegant antique showrooms, the designer clothes shop count increases as you head for the piazza; Missoni knitwear at 97 and Armani at 139 are the major names. Food stores are to the fore in ⑥ **Via della Croce** – **Focacci** at 43 has everything for a picnic hamper. The area's most affordable restaurants are also here – **Otello alla Concordia** at 81 has an ivy-covered courtyard and sprightly service (LL); **Il Re degli Amici**, a long-established eatery, also serves pizzas in the evening (LL); **Beltramme** at 39 is an old-fashioned *osteria*, so well known as to have no name over the door (L). ⑦ **Piazza di Spagna** gets its name from ⑧ the **Palazzo di Spagna**, the Spanish Embassy to the Holy See since the 1700s. The square's set-piece is ⑨ the **Spanish Steps**, one of Rome's Baroque pearls, built in 1726 by Francesco De Sanctis. Properly called the Scalinata di Trinità dei Monti, the sweeping steps are flanked by two monuments to 19thC Britain: ⑩ **Babington's Tea Room** has been serving afternoon tea for nearly a century; and ⑪ the Romantic poet John Keats died in 1821 at the age of 25 in the pink-stuccoed building that now houses the **Keats-Shelley Memorial**. ⑫ At the foot of the steps, the **Barcaccia Fountain** dribbles water from the prow and poop of a sinking ship – a witty solution to low water pressure. ⑬ **Ranieri** (26, Via Mario de' Fiori) was founded in 1865 by Neapolitan Giuseppe Ranieri, one-time chef to Queen Victoria – the luxury restaurant rather rests on its laurels (LLL). ⑭ **Via dei Condotti** is the city's chicest shopping row – Gucci, Valentino and Armani stand shoulder to shoulder in this label hunters' paradise. ⑮ **Caffè Greco** at 86 dates from 1760 – where Goethe, Gogol, Wagner and Liszt once sipped coffee, less distinguished tourists are today served by tail-coated waiters. In ⑯ the **18thC palace** at 68, the Knights of Malta have their headquarters in the world's smallest sovereign state. ⑰ The discreetly opulent **Hotel d'Inghilterra** (14, Via Bocca di Leone) has one of Rome's most romantic dining rooms and an illustrious visitors' book (LLL).

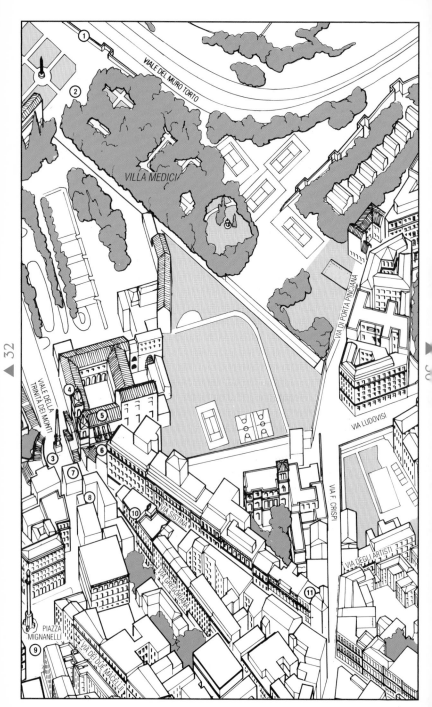

56

Rome's 19thC beau monde once took its evening *passeggiata* or constitutional on the airy heights above the Spanish steps. ① The crooked section of the Aurelian Wall – the **Muro Torto** – forms the ramparts to ② the trim **gardens of the Villa Medici**.The villa itself now houses the National Academy of France. The seductive curves of the Spanish Steps (see page 33) end at ③ **one of Rome's 13 obelisks**; despite the Egyptian hieroglyphs, this one is a Roman pastiche of the 2ndC put here in 1789. The balustraded terrace in front provides a magnificent roof-top view of Rome. The nuns in ④ the **Convento del Sacro Cuore** live their celibate existence where the sybarite Lucullus once feasted Cicero and Pompey.The French King Louis XII ordered the building of ⑤ **Trinità dei Monti** in 1502. Its privileged position promises a more interesting church than it really is – behind the twin-towered, stuccoed façade by Carlo Maderno, the treasures inside are a touch disappointing, though Poussin thought Daniele da Volterra's *Deposition* the third greatest painting in the world. ⑥ Hotel Hassler has played host to the great for more than a century in one of Rome's most outstanding *alberghi* (LLL). Across the piazza, ⑦ the homely **Scalinata di Spagna** has more modestly priced rooms, a warm welcome and a fine view from the roof garden (LL-LLL). Down the steps in Piazza Mignanelli, there are plenty of outdoor tables at ⑧ **Ristorante Alla Rampa** (LL). Across the square, ⑨ an **antique column** stands to celebrate the proclamation in 1854 of the dogma of the Immaculate Conception; in its shadow is a McDonald's hamburger bar. ⑩ On the front of **Palazzetto Zuccari** along Via Gregoriana, recently restored monster masks frame the portal and window of the one-time home of the Queen of Poland. ⑪ Hans Christian Andersen's *The Improvisators* was inspired by his stay at **104, Via Sistina**.

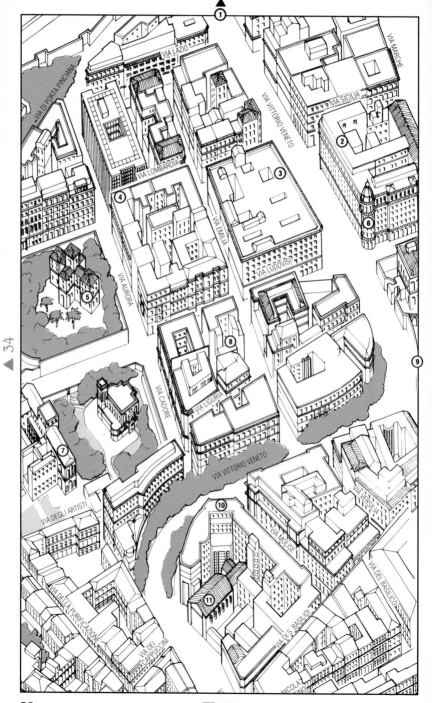

▼ 58

Via Vittorio Veneto

The gardens of the Villa Ludovisi, a famed Roman beauty spot, covered most of this area until the family sold the land for development in 1886. In the 1950s it was the stylish back-drop for Fellini's *La Dolce Vita*, but now much of the glamour has flown. Bland luxury, solid money and dull architecture are all that is left in Via Vittorio Veneto – and Rome's highest count of grand hotels. The presence of the U.S. Embassy may explain its popularity with Americans. ① **Porta Pinciano** (off map), the ancient gateway that pierces the Aurelian Wall to the north, brings the thoroughfare to an abrupt halt. ② **Doney**, on the so-called `American' side of the street, vies with ③ the **Café de Paris** opposite for the title of the area's most celebrated bar. ④ Few airs and graces, however, at **Piccolo Mondo** (39, Via Aurora) a jolly restaurant that spills out on to the pavement (LL). ⑤ The **Casino dell'Aurora**, the last vestige of the Ludovisi estate, hides among trees high above the street. ⑥ The **Hotel Excelsior** is the grandest of the grand hotels (LLL). ⑦ A name plate in Gaelic announces **Sant'Isidoro**, once a refuge for Irish monks escaping persecution, now the Irish Franciscan College. ⑧ Refugees from Via Veneto's grand hotels might consider **La Residenza** (22, Via Emilia) – 27 rooms at comparatively down-to-earth prices (LL). ⑨ **Palazzo Margherita** stands on the site of the Villa Ludovisi itself; once home to Queen Margherita of Savoy, it is now the U.S. Embassy. ⑩ The great **bronze doors** of the Ministry of Industry and Commerce date from the more confident days of the early Fascist era. Guido Reni's painting of St Michael in ⑪ the Cappuchin church of **Santa Maria della Concezione** was one of Rome's chief tourist draws in the 19thC. Now the main attraction is the macabre *Coemeterium* under the church. Here the bones of some 4,000 friars have been tastefully arranged in Baroque patterns to decorate the vaults of this underground cemetery. *That which you are, we were; that which we are, you will be*, reads their epitaph in the end chapel. This gloomy thought did little to stop the worldly activities of Friar Pacifico, one of the monastery's 19thC inmates, who was so accurate at foretelling winning lottery numbers that the Pope banished him from Rome.

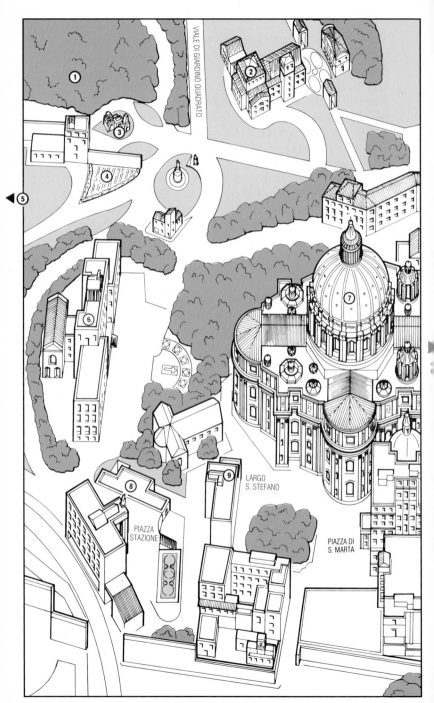

VIALE DI GIARDINO QUADRATO

LARGO
S. STEFANO

PIAZZA
STAZIONE

PIAZZA DI
S. MARTA

The Vatican City

There was a pagan shrine long before Caligula built a circus here. Under Nero, the ring witnessed the martyrdom of St Peter, crucified upside-down around AD 67 and buried in a nearby cemetery. Over his bones stands the Vatican City, a sovereign state since the Lateran Treaty of 1929 between Mussolini and the Holy See. As well as earning pin money from printing its own stamps, it mints its own coinage, publishes its own newspaper, has a mere 550 citizens, uses Latin as its official language, has a diplomatic court drawn from 112 countries and closes its gates punctually at 11 pm. There are two ways for ordinary tourists to see the Vatican Gardens that cover the hill behind St Peter's – either as a bird's-eye-view from the top of the dome or on the two-hour guided tour (daily at 10 am; book in advance with your passport at the Vatican information office in St Peter's Square). ① The shady walks of the English Garden were a favourite morning haunt of Pope John XXIII during his short four-year reign. ② The little 16thC **Casina** of Pius IV is the most pleasing building in the gardens. The rustically decorated summer house is now the seat of the Vatican Academy of Science. ③ The Borghese family eagle tops the high cascade of the **Fontana dell'Aquilone**, the waterhead for all other fountains in the Vatican. ④ An incongruous *orto* or vegetable garden provides fruit and vegetables for the Pope's lonely table. ⑤ **Vatican Radio** (off map) spreads the word in 35 languages; nearby is the French Government's gift of a concrete facsimile of the Grotto of Lourdes, built into the restored ruins of Leo IV's 9thC walls. The more modern walls that encircle the city were built by Michelangelo. ⑥ The **Palazzo del Governatorato**, the gardens' most obvious building, houses the Vatican's civil administration, ruled over by the Cardinal Secretary of State. The gardens provide the finest view of ⑦ Michelangelo's **dome of St Peter's**; the tradition not to build anything higher in Rome is still respected. In its shadow, the Sistine Chapel (see page 41), the seat of the Papal elections, stands in isolation from the rest of the Vatican Palace, more a fortress than a church. ⑧ The **Vatican railway station** is so little used, and then only for goods, that the upper storey has been converted into a stamp and coin museum. ⑨ A reminder that the Vatican is a law unto itself, the **Palazzo di Giustizia** metes out justice for minor offences.

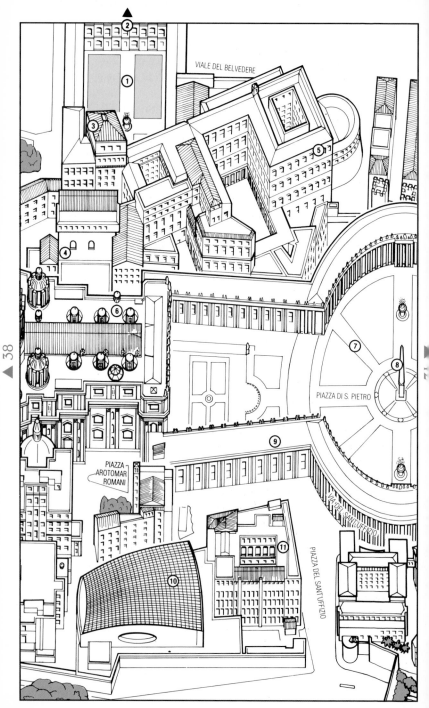

VIALE DEL BELVEDERE

PIAZZA DI S. PIETRO

PIAZZA AROTOMAR ROMANI

VIALE DEL SANTUFFIZIO

PIAZZA DEL SANTUFFIZIO

St Peter's and the Vatican Museums

The labyrinth of chambers, galleries, courts and staircases of the Vatican palaces span some 350 years of feverish building work started in the 15thC. Much of it now houses ① the **Musei Vaticani** – such a dazzling collection that it now needs a 'traffic control' system to cope with the crowds. The **entrance** is ② off the map in Viale Vaticano – follow signs from St Peter's Square or board Vatican bus from ⑨. Take the shortest, violet colour-coded itinerary to see the star attractions – the legendary antique sculptures of the **Laocoön** and the **Apollo Belvedere**; the frescoes in ③ the **Raphael Stanze**; and ④ the **Sistine Chapel**. Modern Popes live in ⑤ former servants' quarters behind the two right-hand windows on the top floor of the tall *palazzo* – on Sunday mornings, John Paul II appears at his window to pray with the crowds. ⑥ **The Basilica of St Peter** is the world's greatest church only in size and historical association. It took more than a century and most of the greatest 16thC architects in Rome to put together this conglomeration of a church: the lack of one single guiding genius shows. Inside, Michelangelo's sculpture of the Pietà (1500) puts the megalomaniac grandeur of the rest in the shade. No lack of genius, either, in ⑦ Bernini's immense, elliptical **Piazza San Pietro** surrounded by his triumphant sweeping colonnades – the welcoming arms of Mother Church or the tentacles of a rapacious octopus, depending on your point of view. ⑧ The Vatican Obelisk, once a centrepiece in Nero's Circus where St Peter was martyred, stood in its ancient position to the left of the basilica until 1586. It took four months and 900 men to move it out front to the centre of the piazza. Once topped by a gilded globe, said in medieval times to contain the ashes of Julius Caesar, it is now more appropriately crowned with a reliquary containing a piece of the True Cross. Between the obelisk and either of the noble fountains, hunt out the round white stones set in the pavement – from here the 284 columns of the colonnades resolve into a single row. ⑨ The **Vatican Information Office**, Post Office, bus stop for the museums and free lavatories serve the secular needs of pilgrims and tourists. ⑩ Pier Luigi Nervi's bold **Papal Audience Hall**, finished in 1971, holds 12,000 for the weekly Papal Audiences. ⑪ Behind the grimy 1925 façade of the **Palazzo del Sant'Uffizio**, lies the older building of the Holy Office, the court of final appeal for heretics in the days of the Inquisition.

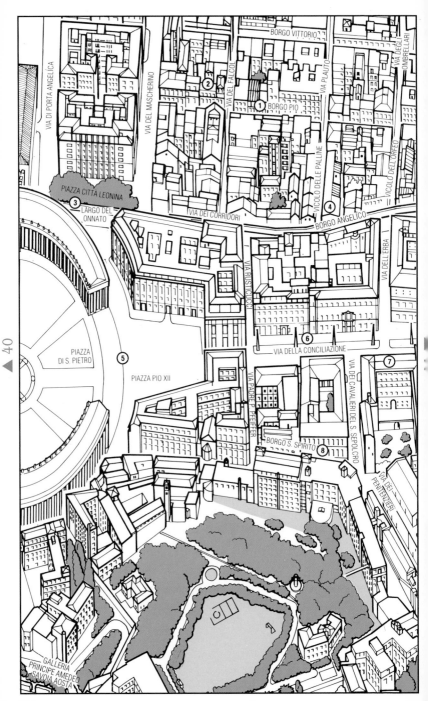

The Borgo

Around Constantine's original basilica of St Peter (later replaced by the present one), Saxons, Franks and Lombards built hostels and chapels for their pilgrims, giving the Germanic word Burg, now Borgo, to the area. The great fire in 847 destroyed this Gothic enclave (Raphael vividly portrays the event in one of his *Stanze* – frescoed rooms – in the Vatican) and any traces of its former occupants were finally erased in its medieval restoration. Today, it is a surprising backwater, a mitre's toss from St Peter's. ① **Borgo Pio** seems furthest away from the tourist droves, with ironmongers and old-fashioned grocery shops vying with cheap *pizzerie* and bars. ② The recently restored **Hotel Sant'Anna** (133, Borgo Pio) is one of the prettiest small *alberghi* this side of the Tiber (LL). ③ A fortified corridor, *il passetto*, runs along the top of the old walls from the Vatican to the safety of Castel Sant'Angelo. Earlier popes took care to keep it well repaired; in 1527, it provided Clement VII with a timely escape route during the sack of Rome. ④ In its shadow, the cheap and cheerful **Bramante Hotel** (24, Vicolo delle Palline) huddles in amongst ancient carpenters' workshops (L). ⑤ The **barriers** at the start of Piazza San Pietro mark the official frontier of the Vatican State. The Borgo once spread across ⑥ **Via della Conciliazione** (see page 45) until Mussolini's bulldozers moved in during the 1930s. ⑦ A hotel fit for a cardinal but at reasonable prices, the **Columbus** (33, Via della Conciliazione) is housed in the Renaissance Palazzo dei Penitenzieri (LL). ⑧ The spirit of **Borgo Santo Spirito** is unquiet, troubled by a flood of traffic. To the south lies a no-man's-land of Vatican offices.

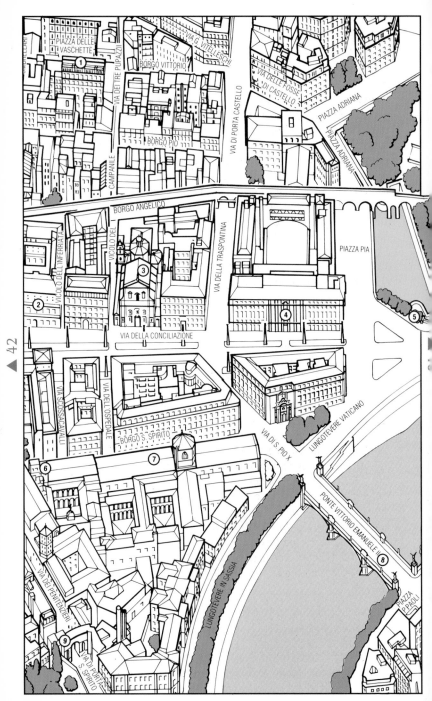

Via della Conciliazione

The idea of a grand ceremonial approach to St Peter's goes back to the 15thC, but it was only in the wake of the conciliation between Church and State in 1929 that the road builders actually began work. Some regard Via della Conciliazione as a fitting overture to the great basilica, others as an act of vandalism whose creation ripped out the heart of the medieval Borgo (see page 43). The road itself is a forbidding, lifeless motorway with broad, vacant pavements. ① Away from the traffic in a little piazza on Borgo Vittorio, the **Taverna Angelica** (14, Piazza delle Vaschette) serves serious food in a tasteful dining room (LL). ② The considered elegance of the travertine Renaissance **Palazzo Torlonia** stands out in the architectural mess of Via della Conciliazione. In the years leading up to the English Reformation, it was the seat of Henry VIII's Ambassador to the Papacy, entrusted with the thankless task of negotiating the English King's divorce. ③ Worldly expedience came before aesthetics when the Baroque church of **Santa Maria in Traspontina** was built: the dome was erected without a drum in order to give a clear field of fire from nearby Castel Sant'Angelo. ④ A modern concert hall, the **Auditorium di Palazzo Pio**, holds an audience of 2,800. ⑤ On a lonely patch of grass (off map) stands the preoccupied figure of **Santa Caterina**, the Protectress of Italy. Only the name of ⑥ the little church of **Santo Spirito in Sassia** recalls its English connections: it was here that the Saxon King Ine of Wessex founded the Burgus Saxonum in 726 as a refuge for the weary pilgrims from his homeland. Inside, it is a contemplative retreat from the razzle-dazzle of St Peter's. ⑦ The adjoining **hospital of Santo Spirito in Sassia** is still in use. The long, arcaded façade on Borgo Santo Spirito, topped by an unusual octagonal drum, dates from the late 15thC. ⑧ One glance tells you that the **Ponte Vittorio Emanuele II** is of modern construction – the clumsy heaviness of the statuary is pitiful beside Bernini's work on the nearby Ponte Sant'Angelo (see page 47). Brave the traffic, though, for a splendid view as far as the Pincio and across to the Janiculum Hill. ⑨ The sturdy Cinquecento gateway of the **Porta Santo Spirito** marks the limits of the Borgo.

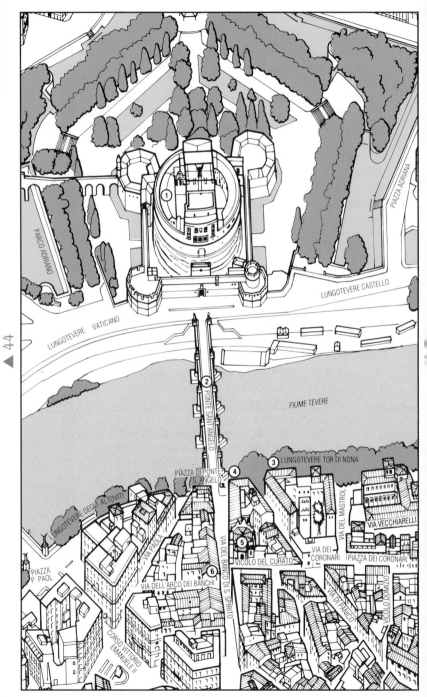

PARCO ADRIANO

PIAZZA ADRIANA

LUNGOTEVERE CASTELLO

LUNGOTEVERE VATICANO

PONTE SANT'ANGELO

FIUME TEVERE

LUNGOTEVERE TOR DI NONA

PIAZZA DI PONTE S. ANGELO

LUNGOTEVERE DEGLI ALTOVITI

VIA DEI MASTROL

VIA VECCHIARELLI

VIA PAOLA

VIA DEI CORONARI

PIAZZA DEI CORONARI

VICOLO DEL CURATO

PIAZZA P. PAOL

VIA DEL BANCO DI S. SPIRITO

VIA DELL'ARCO DEI BANCHI

VIA DI PANICO

VICOLO DOMIZIO

CORSO VITTORIO EMANUELE II

68

Castel Sant'Angelo

Thomas Hobbes's description of the Papacy as 'the ghost of the deceased Roman Empire sitting crowned upon the grave thereof' takes on a chilling aptness at one of Rome's most famous monuments. For the fortress of Castel Sant'Angelo that witnessed so many of the excesses of the powerful medieval popes was originally the mausoleum of the Emperor Hadrian. Begun in 130, it housed the ashes of succeeding Roman emperors until Septimius Severus. ① The **Castel** itself, at least from the waist down, is still essentially Hadrian's, though the lavish marble cladding has long since gone. Inside, an ancient ramp still leads up to his funerary chamber while above you can visit the luxurious Papal apartments. The bronze angel on its pinnacle and the castle's name record Pope Gregory the Great's vision of an angel sheathing its bloody sword that marked the end of the plague in 590. The castle also enjoyed notoriety as a prison – Benvenuto Cellini was one of the luckier inmates who managed to escape, breaking his leg in the process. A less successful exit was made by Tosca, who brings Puccini's opera to a close by throwing herself off the battlements. Bernini's blithe angels escort you across ② the traffic-free **Ponte Sant'Angelo**, providing a theatrical *mise en scène* for the castle. Three of the original arches of Hadrian's Pons Aelius still carry the weight. ③ The great monoliths of marble needed to build Imperial Rome were unloaded at wharves whose remains lie buried under the modern embankment. ④ **Piazza Ponte Sant'Angelo** was cleared by Pope Nicholas V after 200 pilgrims were crushed to death in a bottleneck on the bridge during the 1450 Holy Year. It was later used as a place of public execution. Rome's Methodist Church keeps a low profile at No. 3. ⑤ The 5thC church of **Santi Celso e Giuliano** was entirely rebuilt in 1733. The corpses from the 1450 bridge disaster were laid out here. ⑥ Under the covered passageway of **Arco dei Banchi**, the oldest flood level marker in Rome records the inundation of the Tiber in 1277. The Renaissance banking plutocrat Agostino Chigi had his counting house here. In the reign of Pope Julius II, the papal tiara was left with him as security against a loan to help with the building of St Peter's.

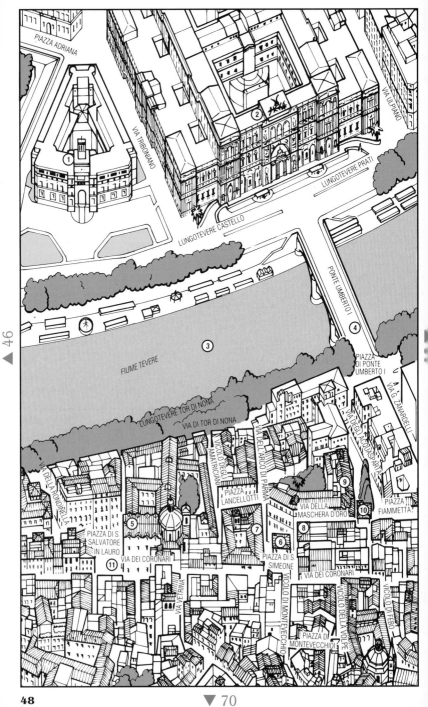

PIAZZA ADRIANA

VIA TRIBONIANO

VIA ULPIANO

LUNGOTEVERE PRATI

LUNGOTEVERE CASTELLO

PONTE UMBERTO I

PIAZZA DI PONTE UMBERTO I

VIA G. ZANARDELLI

FIUME TEVERE

LUNGOTEVERE TOR DI NONA

VIA DI TOR DI NONA

VIA DELL'ARCO DI PARMA

VIA DEGLI ACQUASPARTA

VICOLO DEGLI AMATRICIANI

VIA DELLA RONDINELLA

PIAZZA LANCELLOTTI

VIA DELLA MASCHERA D'ORO

PIAZZA FIAMMETTA

PIAZZA DI S. SALVATORE IN LAURO

VIA DEI CORONARI

PIAZZA DI S. SIMEONE

VIA DEI CORONARI

VIA VETRINA

VICOLO DI MONTEVECCHIO

VICOLO DELLA VOLPE

VICOLO DI FEBO

PIAZZA DI MONTEVECCHIO

① Piacentini's medieval allusions in his 1920's **'fortress'**, built for the National Association for the War Wounded, skilfully echo Castel Sant'Angelo. ② The allusions next door at the **Palazzo di Giustizia** are far from subtle. Calderini's law courts, built in 1910, were an ungainly attempt at the grand gesture so beloved of post-Unification architects. Known to Romans as *il Palazzaccio* – the ugly pile – it has recently needed major works to stop it sinking under the weight. ③ Il Tevere, the **River Tiber**, marked the western boundary of ancient Rome. It is said to be so polluted that a mouthful of its water is fatal – back in 1510, Martin Luther noted the rubbish along the river bank piled twice as high as a soldier's spear. Centuries of flooding was finally bought under control in the 19thC by the building of the Lungotevere embankments. ④ **Ponte Umberto I** (1895). ⑤ A grove of bay trees that stood here in Classical times is recalled in the name of the neo-Classical church of **San Salvatore in Lauro**. ⑥ The comely little **Piazzetta San Simeone**, with its plashing fountain built by Della Porta in 1589, is watched over by the travertine portico of ⑦ the late 16thC **Palazzo Lancellotti**. From the arrival of the Italian troops in 1870 to the Lateran Pact in 1929, Prince Lancellotti kept his gates firmly closed in disgust at the new regime. The **Osteria dell'Antiquario** with tables in the square provides a beguiling corner for lunch (LL). ⑧ An **ancient Roman pillar** holds up a corner of the crumbling stuccoed palazzo on Via della Maschera d'Oro. The world's first scientific academy, the Accademia dei Lincei, was founded in 1603 in ⑨ **Palazzo Cesi**. Today it houses Italy's Supreme Military Court. Cesare Borgia's fiery lover, La Fiammetta, lived in ⑩ the dainty little Quattrocento *casa* with a cat-filled loggia on the Piazza Fiammetta. Rosary bead makers once lined ⑪ **Via dei Coronari**. Their place has now been taken by a string of Rome's finest antique dealers.

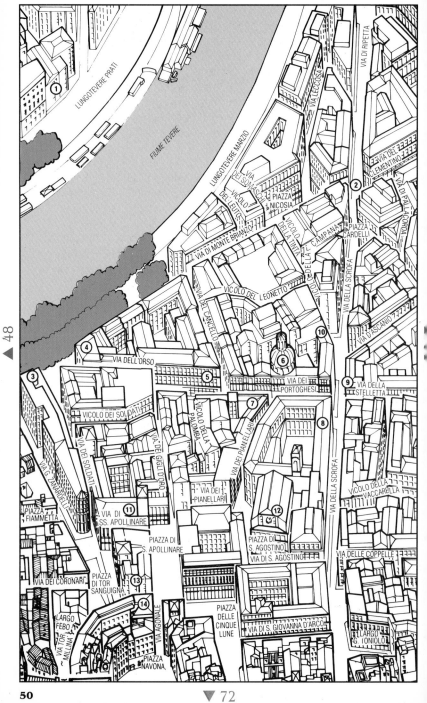

LUNGOTEVERE PRATI

FIUME TEVERE

LUNGOTEVERE MARZIO

VIA DI RIPETTA

VIA LEC COSA

VIA DEI SOMASCHI

VICOLO DELL'EUTICO

PIAZZA NICOSIA

VIA DEI CLEMENTINO

VIA DI PALLACORDA

VICOLO DELLA CAMPANA

VIA DELLA TINTA

PIAZZA CARDELLI

VIA DI MONTE BRIANZO

VICOLO DEL LEONETTO

VIA DEL CANCELLO

VIA DELLA SCROFA

VIA D'ASCANIO

VIA DELL'ORSO

VIA DEI PORTOGHESI

VIA DELLA STELLETTA

VICOLO DEI SOLDATI

VICOLO DELLA PALOMBA

VIA DEI GIGLI D'ORO

VIA DEI PIANELLARI

VIA DELLA SCROFA

VICOLO DELLA VACCARELLA

VIA DEI SOLDATI

VIA G. ZANARDELLI

PIAZZA FIAMMETTA

VIA DI SS. APOLLINARE

VIA DEI PIANELLARI

PIAZZA DI S. APOLLINARE

PIAZZA DI S. AGOSTINO

VIA DI S. AGOSTINO

VIA DELLE COPPELLE

VIA DEI CORONARI

PIAZZA DI TOR SANGUIGNA

LARGO FEBO

VIA TOR MILLINA

VIA AGONALE

PIAZZA DELLE CINQUE LUNE

VIA DI S. GIOVANNA D'ARCO

LARGO G. TONIOLO

PIAZZA NAVONA

① The neo-Gothic church of **Sacro Cuore del Suffragio** hides one of the city's strangest collections, the 19thC **Museo del Purgatorio**. Skull caps, night-shirts, frocks and bibles, fire-branded by the hands of the dead, are said to prove that there is life after death. Across the river, on the threshold of **Piazza Navona** (see page 73), the medieval back streets were once noted for their hostelries. ② From the junction near Della Porta's gracious fountain in Piazza Nicosia, take in the distant view of the obelisks in Piazza del Popolo and Trinità dei Monti. Overlooking the river, ③ **Palazzo Primoli** houses Napoleonic memorabilia in the Museo Napoleonico. Long before Bonaparte, ④ the **Hosteria dell'Orso** was providing hospitality – Rabelais, Montaigne and Goethe were amongst the guests. The porticoed medieval building with recycled ancient columns and capitals is now a flashy restaurant and nightclub (LLL). ⑤ **L'Orso 80** (33, Via dell'Orso) is deservedly popular with Romans (LL). A few doors up, **Il Convivio** (44, Via dell'Orso) is a discreet temple to Roman gastronomy (LLL). ⑥ The florid Baroque face of Rome's Portuguese church, **Sant'Antonio dei Portoghesi**, looks on to a singularly enticing corner of the city. Alongside, the intimate **Hotel Portoghesi** is an inviting *albergo* (LL). Across the narrow street stands ⑦ the mouldering medieval **Torre della Scimmia**. Its odd name, the Tower of the Monkey, recalls the pet ape who carried a new-born baby up to the battlements. In their terror, the infant's parents vowed to keep a light burning to the Madonna if it was returned to safety. The infant was unharmed and the light still burns above. Via della Scrofa – Sow Street – is said to take its name from ⑧ the worn relief of a sow set in the wall; the street now boasts several pork butchers. ⑨ **Volpetti's** (31, Via della Scrofa) is one of Rome's best *salsamenterie* – a superior delicatessen. Up the street, ⑩ **Alfredo all Scrofa** has been serving the best *fettuccine* (Roman ribbon pasta, typically dressed with butter) for more than half a century (LL). ⑪ The distinguished Cinquecento **Palazzo Altemps** is now being given a face lift for its new role as a museum. ⑫ The simple early Renaissance façade of **Sant'Agostino** was built from travertine plundered from the Coloseum. Raphael's *Prophet Isaiah* and Caravaggio's *Madonna of Loreto* adorn the 18thC interior. ⑬ The grimy **Tor Sanguigna** is all that remains of a medieval fortress built by the Sanguigni family. ⑭ Across the square, 7 m below the present street level, a Roman gateway to Domitian's Stadium stands tucked away under a modern insurance office block.

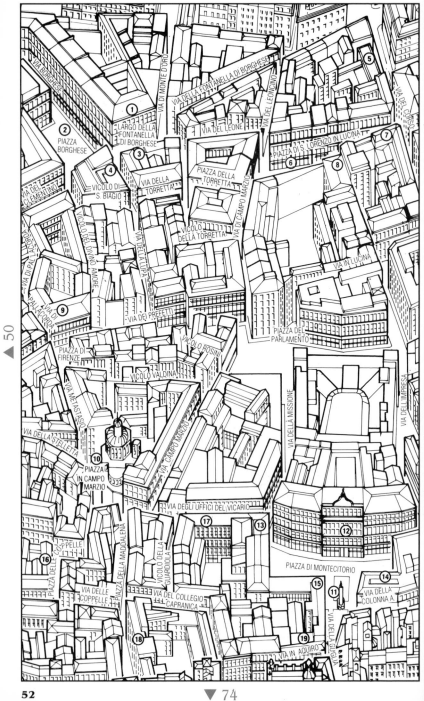

① The princely, harpsichord-shaped **Palazzo Borghese** was famed as the original home of Cardinal Scipione Borghese's fabled art collection, now housed in Villa Borghese (see page 29). ② Thumb through old prints of Rome at the **morning market in Piazza Borghese**. ③ Hearty Tuscan cookery at **La Fontanella** (86, Largo della Fontanella di Borghese, LL). ④ **El Toulà** (296, Via della Lupa) is a voguish and ultra-refined restaurant (LLL). The vast, rusticated face of ⑤ the 16thC **Palazzo Ruspoli** is the work of the Florentine architect Bartolomeo Ammannati. The warm hues of ⑥ the long, narrow **Piazza San Lorenzo in Lucina** make a perfect setting for an ice cream at Ciampini, No.29, or a coffee at Teichner, No.16; more lasting memories from the well-stocked china shop at Tupini, No.10. The Ara Pacis (see page 31) was found under ⑦ **Palazzo Fiano**. To support the palace during the excavations, the ground water had to be frozen. ⑧ Classical fragments decorate the ample porch of the ancient church of **San Lorenzo in Lucina**; inside, all is Baroque. Towering above, the 13thC *campanile* leans away from the Evangelical Baptist church across the square. Behind the polished Florentine façade of ⑨ **Palazzo di Firenze**, once the seat of the Tuscan state in Rome, lives the society dedicated to Florence's greatest son, Dante Alighieri. ⑩ **Piazza Campo Marzio** recalls the Campus Martius, the open, level area used by the Romans for military training in the early days of the city. Rome's founding father, Romulus, vanished here while reviewing his troops in a thunderstorm. A few squat columns bedded in the walls are the only reminder of ancient times. ⑪ A patched-up obelisk, once the pin which cast the shadow for a king-sized sundial, stands unmoved by the goings-on in ⑫ **Palazzo Montecitorio**. Started by Bernini in 1650, the palace now houses the Camera dei Deputati, Italy's lower house of Parliament. The Temple to Marcus Aurelius, Imperial Rome's model statesman, stood on its site. At the rear of the building are some fanciful touches of Italian Liberty style. The visitors' books at the palatial ⑬ **Hotel Nazionale** and ⑭ **Hotel Colonna Palace** read like a political *Who's Who* (both LLL). ⑮ **Herder** (118, Piazza Montecitorio) is Rome's German language bookstore. ⑯ **Da Mario**, hidden away in the crumbling small Piazza delle Coppelle, has fine, unembellished Roman food (LL). ⑰ Rome's much-praised ice-cream parlour, **Giolitti** (42, Via Uffici del Vicariato) has seen better days, but their *gelati* are still hard to beat. ⑱ The façade of **Santa Maria Maddalena** is showy Rococo. ⑲ **Palazzo Capranica**, early Renaissance with an intriguing touch of Gothic, is now a cinema.

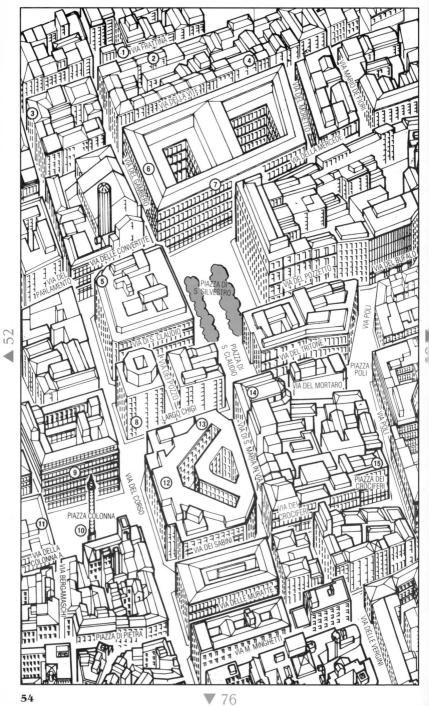

The Corso to Piazza Colonna

① **Via Frattina** is a more approachable shopping street than its genteel neighbours to the north; heading from the Corso, **Fornari** at No.71 stocks unusual modern silver work; **Vanni** across the road serves lunch from an appetising *tavola calda* (L); silk ties galore at **Giofer**, No.118; next door, **Santini's** ultra-modern showroom has a minimalist display of choice bags and shoes; Viennese treats at **Krechel** pastry shop, No.134. ② James Joyce stayed at No.50 - Rome, he reckoned, was like a man who earned his keep 'by exhibiting to travellers his grandmother's corpse'. A century-old temple to sensible dressing, ③ **Schostal** (158, Via del Corso) is where patrician Romans buy their underwear. ④ **Mario** (55, Via della Vite) is another temple, this time to Tuscan cooking (LL). Two doors up is the American Bookshop. In ⑤ the crystal and gilt **Caffè Alemagna** on Via del Corso they have been serving coffee since 1870. Standing on the site of Marcus Aurelius' Temple of the Sun, ⑥ **San Silvestro in Capite** contains the alleged remains of the head of John the Baptist. It has an entrancing courtyard and they say mass in English. In medieval times the monks here made a tidy income from charging pilgrims to climb the nearby Column of Marcus Aurelius. Next door, the well-ordered 19thC façade of ⑦ Rome's **Central Post Office** hides disorder within. ⑧ **La Rinascente** (189, Via del Corso), Rome's largest department store, was baptised 'the reborn' by the poet Gabrielle d'Annunzio in the 1920s when it rose again from the ashes of a fire. ⑨ Behind the spruce late-Renaissance front of **Palazzo Chigi**, just one of the palaces built by Rome's wealthy banking family, the Italian Prime Minister now has his offices. Piazza Colonna, sadly reduced to a government car park, is given dignity by ⑩ the **Column of Marcus Aurelius**. Built in 196, its worn carvings spiral up 30 m to celebrate the philosopher Emperor's campaigns to defend Rome's beleaguered frontiers. Pillars from the Etruscan city of Veii help to hold up the elegant portico of ⑪ **Palazzo Wedekind**, once the Fascist Party headquarters, now the offices of *Il Tempo* newspaper. Across the square, the turn-of-the-century glass arcade of ⑫ the **Galleria Colonna** is looking forward to a face-lift. ⑬ **Rizzoli** is one of Rome's major bookstores. In 1256, an image of the Madonna painted on a stone miraculously floated to the top of a well in ⑭ the church of **Santa Maria in Via** – both stone and well are still inside. It took Gherardi almost 20 years to complete the glorious paintings which embellish the ceiling in ⑮ **Santa Maria in Trivio**.

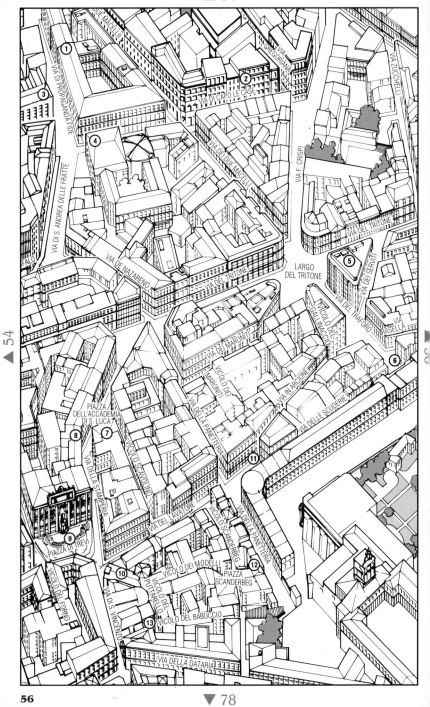

The hand of maverick Baroque architect Borromini is clear in the playful curves of the facade of ① The **Palazzo di Propaganda Fide**, along Via di Propaganda Fide. The Congregation de Propaganda Fide, is the Catholic Church's 'mission control'. ② Exquisite hand-decorated paper at **Papirus** (55, Via di Capo le Case). ③ Gian Lorenzo Bernini, the mastermind behind Baroque Rome, lived on the corner of **Via della Mercede** until his death in 1680. ④ Across the way, in the Scottish church of **Sant'Andrea delle Fratte**, a pair of his angels look down on the florid interior. Borromini's quirky campanile tops it all. Outside ⑤ the **headquarters of Il Messaggero** newspaper, a striking Liberty style, cast-iron news stand sells the latest editions. ⑥ The 350-m **tunnel** on Via Traforo runs under the Quirinal Gardens to Via Nazionale. ⑦ From 1577, young artists learnt their trade at the **Accademia di San Luca**, which was moved here from its site in the Forum in the 1930s. The fine gallery includes work by Raphael, Titian and Rubens (open Mon, Wed, Fri). ⑧ The **Calcografia Nazionale**, an institute dedicated to Italy's major engravers, houses some 24,000 original copper plates. ⑨ The **Trevi Fountain**, Rome's greatest Baroque *coup de théâtre*, is carved into the end wall of Palazzo Poli and fills most of the tiny square in front. Reined in by muscular Tritons, two horses draw an imperious Neptune in his sea-shell chariot while all around water tumbles from every facet. Built in the middle of the 18thC by Nicolò Salvi, it marks the end of the 20-km Roman aqueduct of the Acqua Vergine – named after the young girl who pointed out the source to Agrippa's soldiers back in 19 BC. Last century, visitors drank the waters to ensure their return to Rome; nowadays, the crowds are happier to throw in a coin – those in the know toss them over their left shoulders. ⑩ The church of **Santi Vincenzo e Anastasio**, faced in confident Baroque, was the parish church of the papal Quirinal Palace. Most popes between 1590 and 1903 were borne here to be embalmed and their entrails are still preserved in the crypt. ⑪ Tucked away under the ramparts of the Quirinal are small streets that still boast real, everyday shops, an earthy fruit and vegetable market and several cheap *trattorie* – try **Sora Lucia** (41, Via della Panetteria) for an authentic dish of tripe *alla Romana* (L). ⑫ **Hostaria Piccolo Arancio** (112, Vicolo Scanderbeg), better known to tourists than Sora Lucia, has good food in bright surroundings (LL). ⑬ A coin's throw from the Trevi fountain, the recently-restored **Hotel Trevi** (off map) is an oasis of calm – one of the more charming small hotels in the centre (LL).

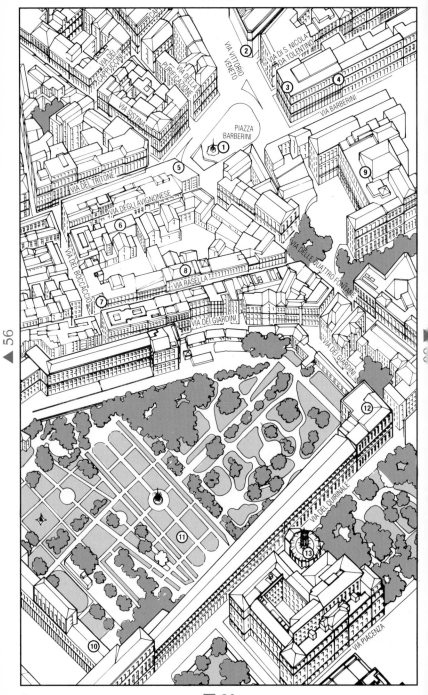

Piazza Barberini

① Centre-stage in **Piazza Barberini**, Bernini's strapping travertine Triton (1643) blows his conch shell to calm the waves of traffic that wash around the square. The bees on the fountain are the family emblem of Bernini's demanding patron, the Barberini Pope Urban VIII. ② At the start of Via Vittorio Veneto, more Barberini bees suck from an open scallop shell in **Bernini's drinking fountain**, built to honour Urban's 22nd year in office. Tempting fate, it was erected a few weeks before the event – the Pope died eight days before his anniversary. ③ The plainest building in the square hides the opulent interior of one of Rome's most luxurious hotels, the **Bristol Bernini** (LLL). ④ Around the corner in Via Barberini, **Cesari** is the place for linen and lingerie while ⑤ **Ceresa** (118, Via del Tritone) has an exhaustive selection of leather goods. ⑥ **Colline Emiliane** (22, Via degli Avignonesi) specializes in the comforting cookery of the Emilia region, home of Parma ham and tortellini (LL). On the 23 March, 1944, 32 German SS soldiers were blown up in a Resistance bomb attack in ⑦ Via Rasella; in revenge, 335 Italians were executed in the Fosse Ardeatine to the south of Rome – the last atrocity in Rome's long history of foreign barbarities. Shrapnel dents still pepper the walls of nearby houses. The top floor of ⑧ the impregnable 16thC **Palazzo Tittoni** briefly served as home to Mussolini. ⑨ The grandiose Baroque pile of **Palazzo Barberini**, completed in 1633 for the Barberini Pope, stood in stately solitude on the side of the Quirinal Hill until the 19thC crept up to its doors. It now houses the Galleria Nazionale d'Arte Antica, a confusing title for a noteworthy collection of Renaissance and Baroque painting including Raphael's *La Fornarina*. ⑩ **The Quirinal Palace**, Gregory XIII's 16thC Papal summer residence, is now the official home of Italy's presidents. Men of modest tastes, they have preferred to live in the smaller ⑫ *palazzetto* that stands at the end of the interminably long, narrow Renaissance wing known as the *manica lunga*, the long sleeve. You will need special permission to get more than a furtive glance at ⑪ the palmy **gardens** from the entrance in Via Quirinale. Heavenly beauty on earth was what the Jesuits wanted in their churches – Bernini came close to it with his masterly design for ⑬ the little oval-domed church of **Sant'Andrea al Quirinale** (1671). Even die-hard critics of Baroque will find it hard not to be swept up in this *tour de force* of gilt and marble. The often self-critical artist thought it one of his finest works.

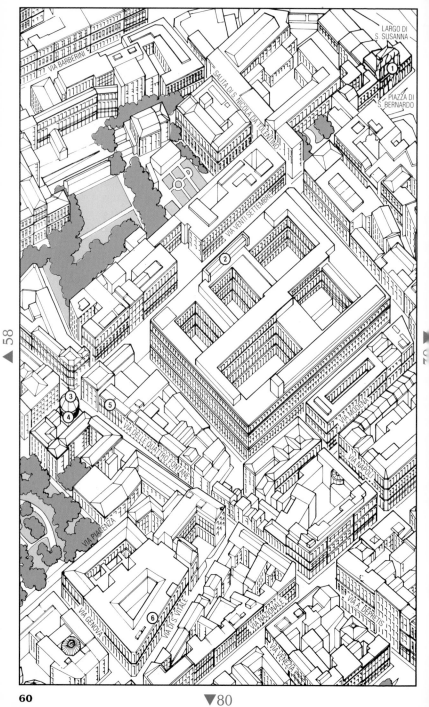

▼80

LARGO DI
S. SUSANNA

①

PIAZZA DI
S. BERNARDO

VIA BARBERINI

SALITA DI S. NICOLA DA TOLENTINO

VIA VENTI SETTEMBRE

②

VIA MODENA

③
④
⑤

VIA DELLE QUATTRO FONTANE

VIA NAPOLI

VIA PIACENZA

VIA DI S. VITALE

VIA GENOVA

⑥

VIA NAZIONALE

VIA A. DEPRETIS

VIA VENEZIA

Quattro Fontane

① The American church of **Santa Susanna** is reputedly built on the spot where its patron was beheaded by Diocletian for refusing the hand of his partner Maximian. Carlo Maderno's Baroque façade (1603) broke new ground in its day. Ponderous 19thC neo-Classical barracks house ② the **Ministry of Defence**, a typical example of the prosaic office development that followed in the wake of Italy's Unification. ③ At the **crossroads of the Quattro Fontane**, the summit of the Quirinal Hill, four discreet fountains bubble from niches in each corner. Three of Rome's obelisks – Trinità dei Monti to the north, the Quirinal to the west and Santa Maria Maggiore to the south – can be seen from here, at least in theory; in practice, you are more likely to be run over than get a reasonable view. ④ In the space taken up by just one of the pillars that support the dome of St Peter's, Borromini created one of his most virtuoso masterpieces, **San Carlo alle Quattro Fontane**. The interior (1638) is a theatrically-lit, architectural game that dazzled his contemporaries. ⑤ The 17thC **Palazzo del Drago** houses the British Council. ⑥ The **Questura Centrale**, Rome's central police station in Via San Vitale, deals with the continual flow of tourists who come to report stolen wallets and handbags.

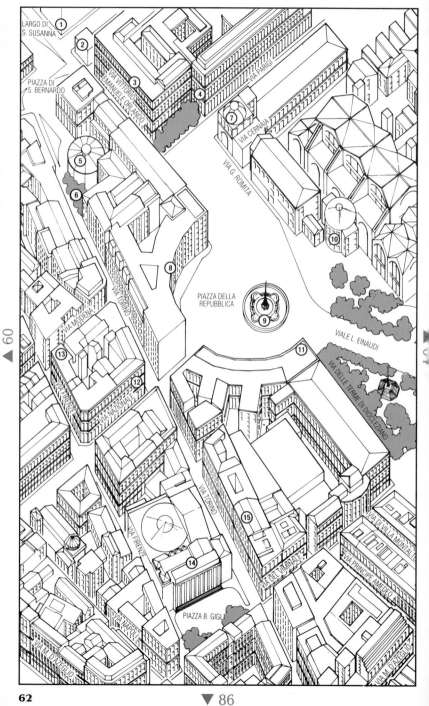

LARGO DI
S. SUSANNA

PIAZZA DI
S. BERNARDO

VIA VITTORIO EMANUELE L. ORLANDO

VIA PARIGI

VIA CERNAIA

VIA G. ROMITA

PIAZZA DELLA
REPUBBLICA

VIALE L. EINAUDI

VIA TORINO

VIA MODENA

VIA TREVIRI

VIA NAZIONALE

VIA DELLE TERME DI DIOCLEZIANO

VIA FIRENZE

VIA TORINO

VIA DEL VIMINALE

VIA DI VILLA MONTALTO

VIA PRINCIPE AMEDEO

VIA M. D'AZEGLIO

VIA NAPOLI

PIAZZA B. GIGLI

VIA M. D'AZEGLIO

The celebrated Cornaro Chapel in ① **Santa Maria della Vittoria** (just off map) frames Bernini's ravishing marble sculpture of the *Ecstasy of St Teresa*. Lit by a shaft of light from above, she is pierced by the spear of Divine Love while the Cornaro family look down in rapt attention from their opera boxes above. ② The **Fontana del Mosè**, built in 1587 to mark the end of the restored Acqua Felice aqueduct, has a grotesque giant statue of Moses. A mischievous story grew up that its creator died of shame at the ridicule it received when unveiled. ③ **Le Grand Hotel** (3, Via V E Orlando) lives up to its name (LLL). ④ One of Rome's three helpful tourist information offices (5, Via Parigi; tel 06-4883748) with plenty of useful hand-outs. ⑤ The Baroque stucco in **San Bernardo** hides the cylindrical building's ancient incarnation as one of the corner rotundas of the vast Baths of Diocletian. Behind the church in Via Torino, ⑥ **Persiani** is a small courtyard shop stuffed with terracotta statuettes and other knick-knacks. ⑦ The octagonal hall from the Roman baths, more recently used as a planetarium and now housing some outstanding ancient bronze statues. ⑧ The lumpen Risorgimento architecture flanking **Piazza della Repubblica** traces the shape of the *exedra*, the curved wall of the stadium in the Baths (see page 65); Romans commonly call it Piazza dell'Esedra. ⑨ The water nymphs that play around the **Fontana delle Naiadi** are reputedly modelled upon a pair of music hall singers; their ample charms caused a scandal when unveiled. Superstitious Romans believe that driving a complete circle round the fountain brings good luck – with a car in Rome you need it. Original Roman masonry from the entrance to the Great Hall of Diocletian's Baths provides the façade to ⑩ the church of **Santa Maria degli Angeli** (see page 65). ⑪ McDonald's hamburger bar caters for young Romans in search of the American Experience and young Americans nostalgic for home (L). ⑫ Another alternative if you tire of Italian food is the Japanese restaurant **Mitsukoshi** on Via Nazionale (LL). Edward Burne Jones created the mosaics in the apse of ⑬ **St Paul's Anglican Episcopal Church**. Behind Piacentini's chaste 1950s façade is the plush 19thC interior of ⑭ the **Teatro dell'Opera**. ⑮ **The Economy Book Store** (136, Via Torino) is Rome's largest English-language bookshop. Next door is the smart **Ristorante Del Giglio** (LL).

Baths of Diocletian

The bones of the Baths of Diocletian, ancient Rome's most monumental *thermae*, sit uncomfortably to the north of the modern mess around the city's main railway station. Completed in 306, they could hold 3,000 bathers at a time. When not sweating in the *calidarium* or cooling off in the *frigidarium*, its patrons could stroll in the gardens, exercise in the gymnasium or browse in the library. ① The cloister of the Carthusian monastery that later grew up amidst the red-brick ruins now forms the centre of the **Museo Nazionale Romano**; entrance at ②. Its arcades, looking like a high-class architectural salvage yard, are lined with ancient sarcophagi, busts and memorial friezes with less than helpful labels. The museum, one of the most important collections of its kind in the world, is in the interminable process of being divided up between new premises (see ⑥ below). The scale of the baths can best be seen in ③ **Santa Maria degli Angeli** (entrance shown on map page 62). As a final revenge for Diocletian's Christian persecutions, Pope Pius IV had Michelangelo convert the great hall of the *tepidarium* into this church. The great artist's respect for antiquity ensured that the glory of its vaulted interior was preserved and, despite Vanvitelli's insensitive tinkering in the 18thC, it is one of the most striking examples of the pagan foundations of Christian Rome. ④ The **Piazza dei Cinquecento** takes its name not from Fiat's answer to the Mini but from 500 Italians killed at Dogali, Eritrea in 1887; their monument, topped by the ubiquitous obelisk, stands in ⑤ the patch of gardens to the west. The enormous piazza is Rome's central bus station and is best avoided at night. ⑥ The spruced-up **Palazzo Massimo** at the side of the square is set to be part of the new Museo Nazionale Romano but at the time of writing it remains firmly closed. Of the numerous uninviting hotels that cluster around the railway station, ⑦ the **Nord** (3, Via G. Amendola) is among the best of a motley bunch (LL).

▲ 64

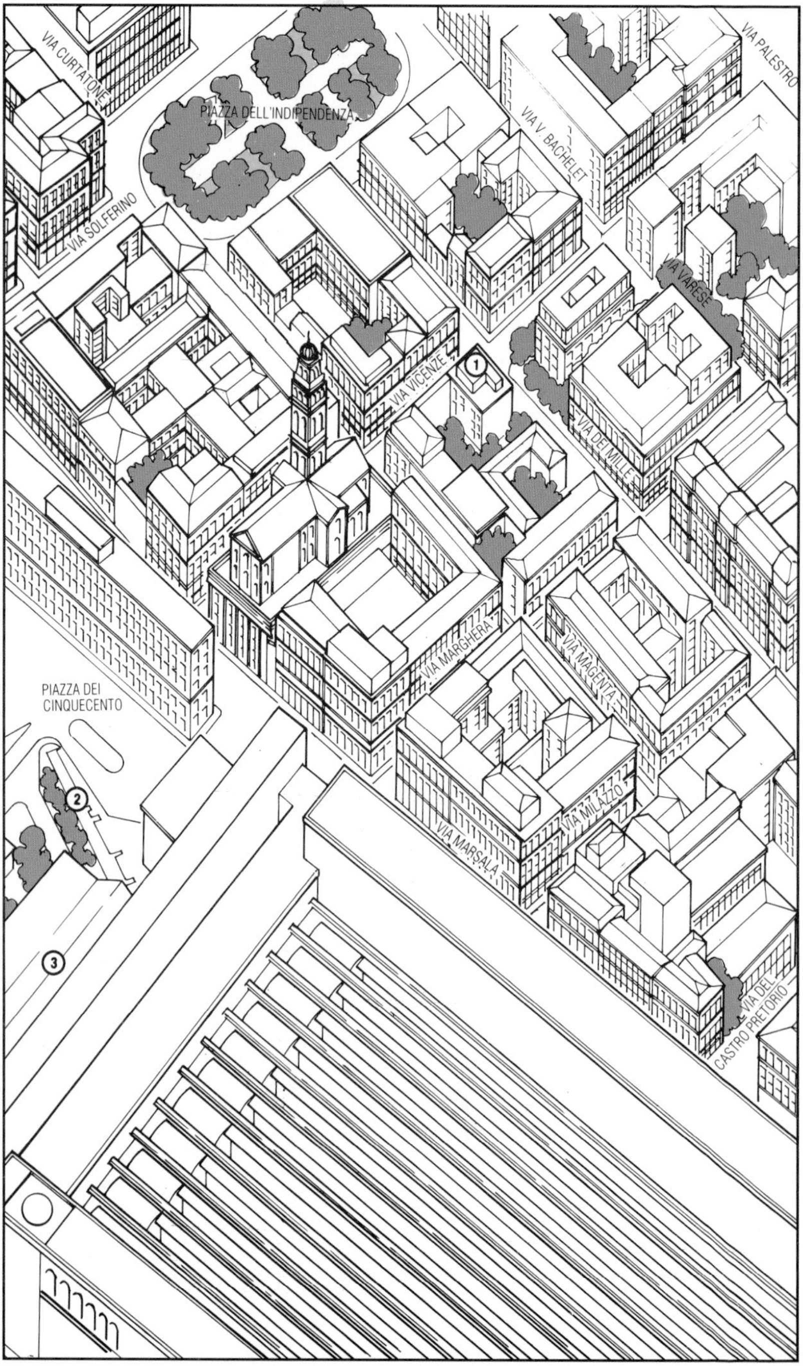

VIA CURTATONE
PIAZZA DELL'INDIPENDENZA
VIA PALESTRO
VIA V. BACHELET
VIA SOLFERINO
VIA VARESE
VIA VICENZE
1
VIA DEI MILLE
VIA MARGHERA
VIA MAGENTA
PIAZZA DEI CINQUECENTO
2
VIA MILAZZO
VIA MARSALA
3
VIA DEL CASTRO PRETORIO

Steer clear of this area unless you have a train to catch: Rome's main railway station attracts the least romantic elements of the city. The characterless late 19thC streets around it have the highest concentration of the city's 850 hotels, but few are inviting. ① **Villa delle Rose** (5, Via Vicenza), a small guest house in an old villa, is a notable exception (L). ② A fragment of Rome's earliest stone defences, the **Servian Wall**, stands unnoticed at the side of the station. Built after the Gauls sacked Rome in 390 BC, it remained the city's main fortification for over 600 years until Aurelius built the great wall that bears his name. One of the handful of inspiring modern buildings in the centre of Rome, ③ **Stazione di Termini** uses concrete with verve. The end of the line for the capital's national and international services, its broad, uncluttered concourse copes comfortably with the crowds. Down below is the interchange between the city's two underground lines, the Metropolitana. The official tourist information office in the station offers more reliable assistance than the touts that haunt the platforms.

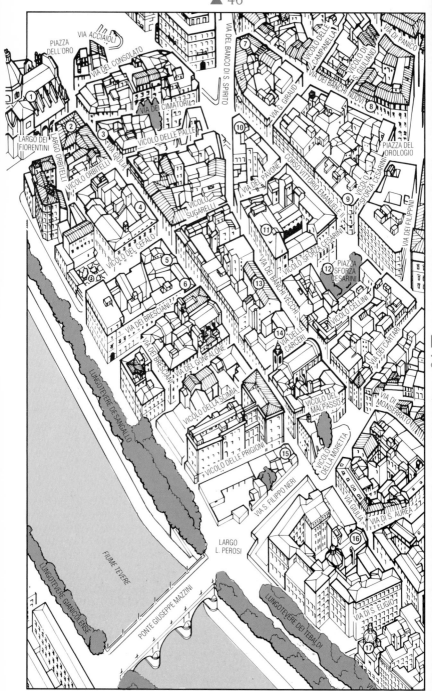

A stately succession of Renaissance palaces distinguishes the one-time centre for Rome's Florentine colony. The dome of their 16thC national church, ① **San Giovanni dei Fiorentini** (off map), looms up over the Tiber. Inside, there is little trace of Florentine artistic genius. ② Sangallo's **Palazzo Medici Clarelli** stands on the threshold of Pope Julius II's ③ **Via Giulia**. Opened in the early decades of the 1600s, the 1-km thoroughfare was the city's first grand gesture in road building since the days of the Roman Empire. Flanked by noble palazzi, it was part of the Pope's masterplan to create a fitting approach to St Peter's and was Renaissance Rome's most prestigious address. ④ The wide, brick façade of the 16thC **Palazzo Sacchetti**. ⑤ The saint still invoked to ward off sore throats is remembered at **San Biagio**. Next door, ⑥ the **Cardinal Hotel** is appropriately red and opulent (LLL). Benvenuto Cellini struck his celebrated medals in the Zecca, Pope Julius II's mint, that stood on the site of ⑦ **Palazzo Zecca**. It now houses the Bank of the Holy Spirit. A sombre medieval atmosphere hangs over ⑧ the narrow **Via de' Banchi Nuovi**, now lined with user-friendly antique shops. In traffic-clogged Corso Vittorio Emanuele II, ⑨ **In Folio**, No 263, has smart presents for executives. Back to a medieval huddle in Via dei Banchi Vecchi: ⑩ **Santucci** is a Noah's Ark of a name-plate shop. Next door, at No 110, **La Riggiola** sells antique tiles. ⑪ **Palazzo Sforza Cesarini** was once compared to Nero's Golden House. It was built for Rodrigo Borgia, the future Pope Alexander VI, who is said to have sold it for the price of Cardinal Ascanio Sforza's vote in the Papal Conclave. Borgia ghosts haunt ⑫ the little **Piazza Sforza Cesarini** – Cesare's and Lucrezia's mother lived at No 27 and the infamous duo may have been born here. Nearby, no frills at **Trattoria Polese**, No 39 (L). Back on Via dei Banchi Vecchi, the ornate stucco-work on ⑬ **Palazzo Crivelli** (No 22-24) is responsible for its nickname, the Doll's House. ⑭ **Il Cardinale** (6, Via delle Carceri) for a warm welcome and a sophisticated rendering of Roman cooking (LL). Brooding over Via Giulia, a secure, no-nonsense brick façade fronts ⑮ Innocent X's **Carcere Nuovi**, considered a model prison when it was built in 1655. The Ministry of Grace and Justice now works behind the heavily-barred windows. The last King of the Two Sicilies lies buried in ⑯ **Spirito Santo dei Napoletani**. A fine dome by Raphael tops ⑰ the goldsmiths' church of **Sant'Eligio degli Orefici** (1516).

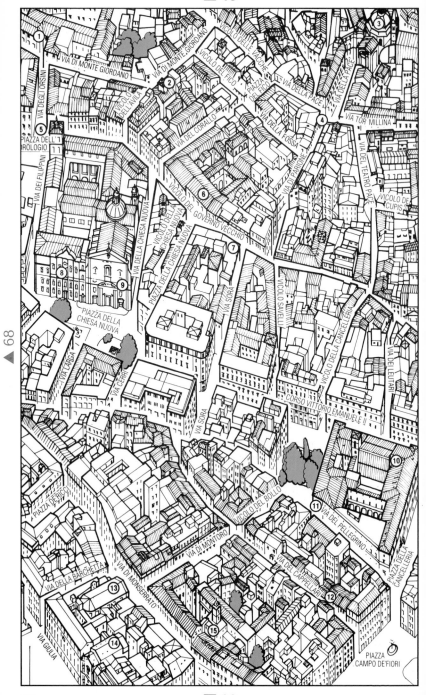

VIA DI MONTE GIORDANO
VIA DEGLI ORSINI
VIA DI MONTE GIORDANO
VICOLO DEL TIGIO
VICOLO DELLE VACCHE
PIAZZA DEL FICO
VIA DELLA PACE
VIA DELLA PACE
VIA TOR MILLINA
VIA DELL'ARCO
PIAZZA DELL'
OROLOGIO
VIA DEI FILIPPINI
VIA DEL CORALLO
VIA DELLA FOSSA
VIA DI PARIONE
VIA DEL TEATRO PACE
VICOLO DE
CUPIS
VICOLO DEL GOVERNO VECCHIO
VIA DELLA CHIESA NUOVA
VICOLO DELLA CHIESA NUOVA
VIA DELLA CHIESA NUOVA
PIAZZA DELLA CHIESA NUOVA
VIA SORA
VIA SORA
VICOLO SAVELLI
VICOLO DELLA CANCELLERIA
VIA DEI LEUTARI
VIA LARGA
VIA CERRI
VIA SORA
CORSO VITTORIO EMANUELE II
PIAZZA DE'RICCI
VICOLO DEL BOLLO
VIA DEL PELLEGRINO
PIAZZA DELLA CANCELLERIA
VIA DELLA BARCHETTA
VIA DI MONSERRATO
VIA DI MONTORO
VIA DEL CAPPELLARI
VIA GIULIA
PIAZZA CAMPO DE'FIORI

1 2 3 4 5 6 7 8 9 10 11 12 13 14 15

Parione

The commanding bulwarks of ① **Palazzo Taverna** crown Via degli Orsini. This one-time palace of the forceful Orsini family is said to be built on the site of Rome's first amphitheatre. ② **Antica Taverna** (12, Via Monte Giordano) has a pretty setting (LL). Rising up at the end of Via di Parione, Pietro da Cortona's eye-catching **porch** (1656) for ③ **Santa Maria della Pace** makes the little square one of Rome's most enchanting retreats. Inside, see the elegantly simple cloisters, Bramante's first work in Rome (1504), and Raphael's fresco of the Sybils. Beware of the bill in the chic bars around ④ Via di Parione, rapidly becoming one of Rome's most modish lanes. Look up from ⑤ **Piazza dell'Orologio** to see Borromini's svelte clock tower (1648). Via del Governo Vecchio was once used for Papal processions from the Lateran Palace to St Peter's. ⑥ The Renaissance **Palazzo del Governo Vecchio** was the seat of the Governors of Rome during the 17thC. ⑦ **Da Baffetto** (11, Via del Governo Vecchio), an institution amongst Roman *pizzerie* (L). Behind Borromini's sinuous brick façade to ⑧ the **Oratorio dei Filippini** is Rome's oldest public library, the **Biblioteca Vallicelliana** (1581). It was from here that St Philip Neri's Oratorians developed the musical form known as the oratorio. Next door, the saint, dubbed 'the Apostle of Rome', lies buried in ⑨ the **Chiesa Nuova**. Around the altar are three fine paintings by Rubens. ⑩ **Palazzo della Cancelleria**, partly built on the proceeds of a night's gambling, is one of the masterpieces of late Quattrocento Rome. Confiscated by Leo X from its original owners, the Riario family, its sobriety and subtle proportions were ideal for its later use as the Papal Chancellery. When Vasari bragged that he had frescoed the great Salone in a hundred days, Michelangelo retorted, "It looks like it". Bramante's church of San Lorenzo, with its splendid gilt coffered ceiling and discreet family balconies in the apse, seems like another grand room in the palace. ⑪ **Via del Pellegrino** (Pilgrim's Way), opened by the unholy Borgia Pope Alexander VI in 1497, was the traditional centre for the city's jewellers. ⑫ Resinous scents from carpenters' workshops linger in medieval **Via dei Cappellari**. In ⑬ the Spanish national church, **Santa Maria di Monserrato**, lies Alfonso XIII, the last King of pre-Civil War Spain. ⑭ **Santa Caterina di Siena** is dedicated to Italy's female patron saint, who persuaded the Papacy to return from Avignon at the close of the 14thC. ⑮ The **Venerable English College**, founded as a hospice for English pilgrims in 1362, claims to be the oldest English institution outside the U.K.

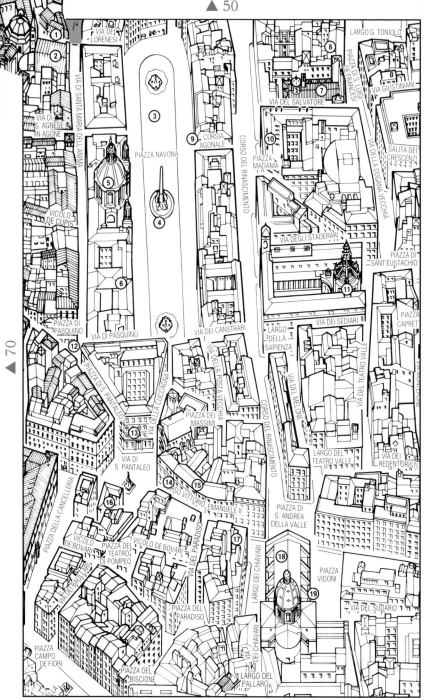

VIA DEI LORENESI

LARGO G. TONIOLO

PIAZZA DI S. LUIGI DE' FRANCESI

VIA GIUSTINIANI

VIA DI S. AGNESE IN AGONE

VIA DI SANTA MARIA DELL'ANIMA

VIA DEL SALVATORE

CORSIA AGONALE

CORSO DEL RINASCIMENTO

SALITA DEI CRESCENZI

PIAZZA NAVONA

PIAZZA MADAMA

VIA DELLA DOGANA VECCHIA

VICOLO DE' CUPIS

VIA DEGLI STADERARI

PIAZZA DI SANT'EUSTACHIO

PIAZZA DI PASQUINO

VIA DI PASQUINO

VIA DEI CANESTRARI

LARGO DELLA SAPIENZA

VIA DEI SEDIARI

PIAZZA CAPRET...

VIA DELLA CUCCAGNA

VIA DELLA POSTA VECCHIA

VIA DEL MELONE

VIA DEI CANESTRARI

VIA DEL TEATRO VALLE

PIAZZA DI S. PANTALEO

PIAZZA DEI MASSIMI

CORSO DEL RINASCIMENTO

VIA DI S. PANTALEO

LARGO DEL TEATRO VALLE

VIA DEI REDENTORISTI

CORSO VITTORIO EMANUELE II

PIAZZA DELLA CANCELLERIA

VIA DEL PARADISO

PIAZZA DI S. ANDREA DELLA VALLE

VICOLO DE' BOVARI

PIAZZA DEL TEATRO DI POMPEO

VICOLO DE' BOVARI

LARGO DEI CHIAVARI

PIAZZA VIDONI

VIA DEL SUDARIO

VIA DE' GIUBBONARI

PIAZZA CAMPO DE' FIORI

PIAZZA DEL BISCIONE

PIAZZA DEL PARADISO

VIA DE' CHIAVARI

LARGO DEL PALLARO

① Creeper-clad **Hotel Raphaël**, one of the city's smartest small hotels (LLL). ② Inside the German church of **Santa Maria dell'Anima** is Peruzzi's magnificent tomb for the 16thC Dutch Pope Hadrian VI: entrance next to Santa Maria della Pace on map page 70. Like a palimpsest, Rome's most exhilarating Baroque square, ③ **Piazza Navona**, preserves the shape of Domitian's stadium of AD 96. Pope Innocent X, seeing to enhance his family name, Pamphilj, (pronounced Pamfili) commissioned the great architects of his day to make the piazza in front of his family home into a fitting memorial to his reign. ④ Bernini's **Fountain of the Four Rivers** (1651) is the piazza's crowning glory colossal figures of the rivers Nile, Danube, Ganges and Plate hold up an ancient Roman obelisk. The restless curves of ⑤ Borromini's **Sant' Agnese in Agone** (1657), where Innocent is buried, upstage the family's ⑥ **Palazzo Pamphilj** next door. Visit ⑦ the 16thC French church of **San Luigi dei Francesi** to see Caravaggio's three masterpieces on the life of St Matthew. To the right of the church is ⑧ **La Procure**, Rome's French language bookshop. On summer evenings fortune tellers line ⑨ **Corsia Agonale.** ⑩ **Palazzo Madama**, provides a suitably superior Seicento building for Italy's Upper House. Borromini's helter-skelter spiral lantern tops ⑪ **Sant'Ivo**, the courtyard church of the **Palazzo della Sapienza**, home to the city's venerable university until 1935. The worn antique torso, called Pasquino, in ⑫ **Piazza Pasquino**, is Rome's most celebrated 'talking statue' – witty comments on the dealings of the high and mighty appear overnight on placards around his neck. ⑬ The grimy **Palazzo Braschi** (1780) houses the **Museo di Roma**, a fascinating documentation of the evolution of the city – pray it is still not 'closed for repairs'. ⑭ A great gash in Rome's history, the **Corso Vittorio Emanuele II** flattened whole tracts of the old city when it was built in 1881. The striking curved portals of ⑮ **Palazzo Massimo alle Colonne** (1536) follow the line of the auditorium of an ancient Roman theatre. Across the street, ⑯ the 16thC **Piccola Farnesina** makes a fine setting for the **Museo Barracco**, a notable collection of antique sculpture. ⑰ For salads, head for **L'Insalata Ricca** (85, Largo di Chiavari), (L). The symmetry of ⑱ **Sant'Andrea della Valle**'s noble pediment (1665) is upset by a single angel – piqued by the Pope's criticism, its sculptor, Fancelli, refused to make its partner. The magnificent gilded interior provides the setting for the first act of Puccini's *Tosca*. ⑲ The statue of an unknown Roman orator with an ancient smirk and full dress toga, nicknamed **Abate Luigi**, is another of the city's 'talking statues'.

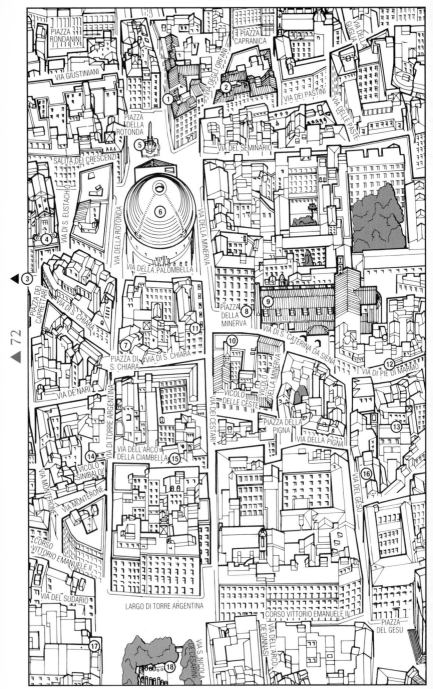

① The venerable **Albergo al Sole** (63, Piazza della Rotonda) has rooms named after its famous guests from Ariosto to Sartre (LLL). Stiff competition between ② **Tazza d'Oro** (Via degli Orfani) and ③ **Bar Sant' Eustachio** (off map) for the best *espresso* in town. Across the square ④ **Sant'Eustachio** is dedicated to the patron saint of the hunt – the cross on the front is framed by antlers. Two lonely pillars at the side of the church are all that remain of the Terme Alessandrine, baths built by Nero in AD 62. ⑤ Della Porta's sparkling fountain (1578), topped by a diminutive obelisk, sits in a sea of bar umbrellas in **Piazza della Rotonda**. The august granite columns of ⑥ the **Pantheon**, the most perfectly preserved building of Ancient Rome, overshadow it. Rebuilt by Hadrian around 120 – with typical modesty he left the name of Agrippa, the builder of the original temple, on the pediment – its dedication as a Christian church in 609 guaranteed its preservation. Under the great dome, the world's widest until this century, Raphael and the first two kings of Italy are buried. ⑦ The **Teatro Rossini** specializes in Roman dialect theatre. Bernini's jolly **pygmy elephant** carries a 6thC BC obelisk on its howdah in ⑧ Piazza della Minerva. Inside ⑨ **Santa Maria sopra Minerva**, Rome's only Gothic church (1280), Santa Caterina lies in state guarded by Michelangelo's heroic sculpture of *Christ the Redeemer*. ⑩ **Palazzo Conti**, where Stendhal stayed, is now a Holiday Inn (LLL). Of the numerous ecclesiastical emporiums here, the well-dressed cleric heads for ⑪ **Gammarelli**, vestment makers to the Pope. ⑫ In Via Pié di Marmo, past a row of imaginative small shops, stands a surreal **marble foot** from a colossal antique statue. ⑬ The 9thC church of **Santo Stefano del Cacco** was built where Romans once worshipped the Egyptian gods Isis and Serapis. ⑭ Fine Ligurian food at **Girone VI** (2, Vicolo Sinibaldi), (LLL). ⑮ The curved wall of the **Terme di Agrippa**, the oldest baths in Rome, is hard to spot amongst the buildings that have grown up around it in Via Arco della Ciambella. ⑯ **Chianti Corsi** (88, Via del Gesù), an old-fashioned wine shop with tables at the back (L). ⑰ **Teatro Argentina**, one of Rome's premier theatres, saw the disastrous first night of Rossini's *Barber of Seville* in 1816. ⑱ The four unidentified temples in **Largo Argentina** – still a riddle to experts – are rare remnants of Republican Rome brought to light in the 1920s.

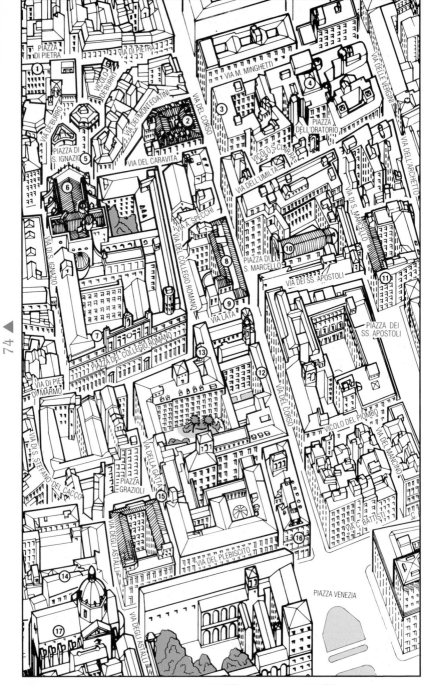

The Corso to Piazza Venezia

Stately palaces, which only banks can now afford to inhabit, and Rome's Jesuit enclave, mark the southern end of the Corso. ① **Eleven marble columns** facing Piazza di Pietra are the vestiges of a temple dedicated in 145 to Emperor Hadrian. The sturdy Mannerist rustication of ② the **Banco di Roma** is a 19thC counterfeit. Behind ③ the sober, late Renaissance **Palazzo Sciarra-Colonna** lies ④ **Galleria Sciarra**, a glass-roofed courtyard with Art Nouveau murals that leave little doubt as to the duties of a well-bred 19thC woman. Little pastel-stuccoed Rococo palaces (1728), nicknamed 'the writing desks', frame ⑤ the winsome little **Piazza Sant'Ignazio** and provide a suitable overture to ⑥ **Sant'Ignazio**. Its exquisite ceiling, painted in 1685 by the Jesuit Andrea Pozzo, is a conjuring trick of *trompe l'oeil* painting best viewed from the disc in the nave. Hemmed in by streets of tall *palazzi*, ⑦ the late 16thC Jesuit **Collegio Romano** educated the sons of Rome's patrician families and a number of future popes. ⑧ Chateaubriand, as French ambassador, stayed in this stern palace long before the **Banco di Roma** acquired it. The broken-nosed figure of ⑨ *Il Facchino* – the porter – on a little fountain is another of Rome's garrulous 'talking statues'. The foundations of ⑩ **San Marcello** date back to the 4thC, though it is hard to guess it from Fontana's heavy Baroque façade (1682). The body of Cola di Rienzo – the 14thC revolutionary whose ill-fated attempt to rekindle Republicanism in Rome inspired Wagner's opera – was strung up outside. ⑪ The neat Baroque **Palazzo Balestra** housed the banished British royal family of the Stuarts from the birth of Bonny Prince Charlie in 1720 to the death of his brother, Henry, Cardinal of York. Behind the vast Rococo façade (1734) of ⑫ **Palazzo Doria Pamphilj** is a worthwhile art collection including works by Titian, Tintoretto and Velasquez – entrance at ⑬; open Tues, Fri, Sat, Sun. Romans had much to say on the unseemly grandeur of ⑭ Clement X's 17thC **Palazzo Altieri**. ⑮ An ancient **stone cat**, unearthed in the nearby temple to Isis, perches up on a cornice in Via della Gatta – buried treasure is said to lie where its gaze falls. Napoleon's mother, Letizia Ramolino, died in 1836 in the slim, ochre-fronted ⑯ **Palazzo Bonaparte**. Begun by Vignola in 1568, ⑰ the church of **Il Gesù** was the prototype for 'Jesuit Baroque'. Riding the waves of the Counter-Reformation, the evangelical Jesuits aimed to stupify their large congregations with splendour. Inside, the tomb of the Order's founder, St Ignatius, staggers under its weight of gold and the world's largest piece of lapis lazuli.

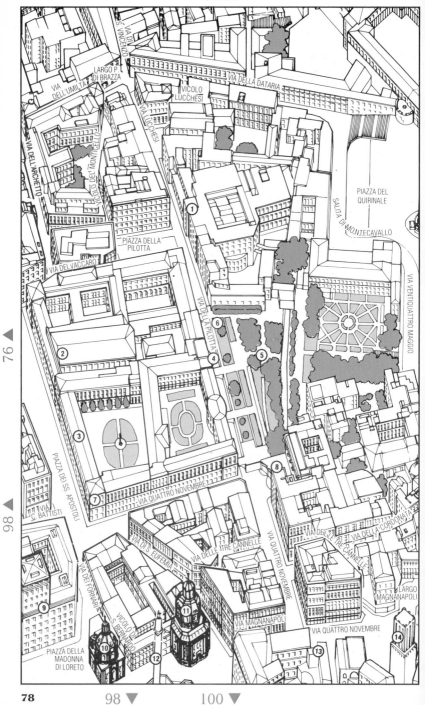

Trajan's Column

On the lower slopes of the Quirinal Hill stands ① the forbidding 1930s building of the **Pontificia Università Gregoriana**. Founded by St Ignatius in 1551, it was later endowed as a university by Gregory XIII, the Pope remembered for introducing the modern Gregorian Calendar. Piazza Santi Apostoli is dominated by the architectural jumble of ② **Santi Apostoli**, an ancient church that the builders could not leave alone. The sweeping balustraded portico, topped by statues of the 12 apostles, is the best part. Most of rambling **Palazzo Colonna** ③ dates from rebuilding in 1730; its low-key art collection is only open Saturday mornings. Its entrance ④ is in Via della Pilotta, a narrow mews spanned by footbridges linking the palace to ⑤ its gardens. Under one of the bridges hides ⑥ **Moriondo & Gariglio**, a tiny shop with the best chocolates in Rome. An outlying corner of the palace serves as home for, among others, Napoleon, Snow White, Oscar Wilde and Hitler in ⑦ Rome's **Waxwork Museum**, the Museo delle Cere. The view up Via IV Novembre is overshadowed by the lofty 19thC gateway to ⑧ a palazzo housing INAIL, an insurance institute. ⑨ A modern mock Venetian palace, echoing Palazzo Venezia across the way (see page 99), houses the Rome offices of **Assicurazioni Generali di Venezia**, the world's oldest insurance company. A plaque records that the house where Michelangelo lived and died once stood on this site. A curious lantern, nicknamed the 'cricket's cage' tops the dome of ⑩ the early 16thC **Santa Maria di Loreto** while the Madonna is again invoked at ⑪ **Il Santissimo Nome di Maria**, this time to commemorate the victory over the Turks by the Polish King Sobieski at the Liberation of Vienna (1683). The posing statues high on the dome of the church have the best view of ⑫ **Trajan's Column**, one of the most telling monuments surviving from Classical times. Around 2,500 figures spiral up the 40-m column to give an action-packed record of the Emperor's Dacian campaigns. The 18 marble blocks were originally coloured and crowned by a statue of Trajan; St Peter took his place in 1587. An evocative reminder of everyday life in ancient times, **Trajan's Market** ⑬ is remarkably intact. This three-tier 'shopping mall' dug into the flank of the Quirinal Hill was built around 112 AD and looks out on to the great apse of Trajan's Forum (see page 101). ⑭ **Torre delle Milizie**, the largest of Rome's remaining medieval towers, leans drunkenly beside it.

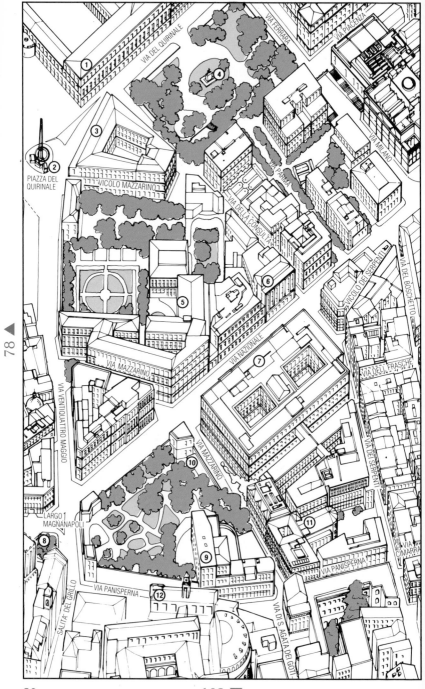

Piazza del Quirinale

When Rome was in its infancy, the Sabine tribes had their stronghold on the Quirinal – the highest of the Seven Hills – and their war god Quirinus is remembered in its name. Facing ① the Quirinal Palace (see page 59) stands the **Dioscuri**, the heroic centre-piece to ② **Piazza del Quirinale**. The colossal statues of the two horse-tamers Castor and Pollux came from the nearby Baths of Constantine, the obelisk from the Mausoleum of Augustus and the granite bowl of the fountain from the Roman Forum. Take a glance at a 500-lire coin if you think the scene is familiar. To the west of the square is a balcony view of Rome with St Peter's framed by TV aerials while opposite is ③ the 18thC **Palazzo della Consulta**, Italy's Constitutional Court, which sits behind Fuga's splendid white façade. ④ An heroic equestrian **statue to King Carlo Alberto**, father of United Italy's first monarch, rules over a pocket-handkerchief park. The sticky sentimentality of Guido Reni's work was much beloved by 19thC tourists who came in droves to see his frescoes (1614) in ⑤ the **Casino Pallavicini**, part of the complex of Palazzo Pallavicini-Rospigliosi (open 1st of each month; entrance at 43, Via XXIV Maggio). The palace's outstanding picture gallery is closed to the general public. ⑥ The two modern auditoria of the **Teatro Eliseo** on traffic-choked Via Nazionale host some of Rome's best drama. Across the road, the heavy, four-square bastion of ⑦ the **Banca d'Italia** (1904) adds its weight in support of the Italian Lira. A few blocks of the ancient Servian Wall lie in the centre of ⑧ the roundabout of **Largo Magnanapoli**. ⑨ **Villa Aldobrandini** was the centre for Roman high society in Napoleonic times. The gardens, perched high above the surrounding streets, have recently been restored and opened to the public; from the shade of citrus trees this little oasis has grandstand views across to the Janiculum Hill. Its entrance is at ⑩, up steps through the few remnants of the Baths of Constantine on Via Mazzarino. A hidden side entrance from Via Panisperna takes you into ⑪ **Sant'Agata dei Goti**, a beguiling church in the form of a tiny basilica that still retains traces of its ancient origins. A fine Baroque stairway leads up to the balustraded entrance to ⑫ the richly decorated church of **Santi Domenico e Sisto** (completed 1655).

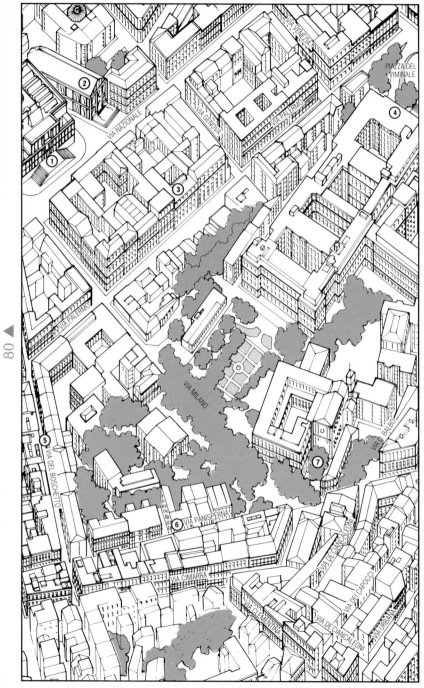

The Viminal Hill

Time has ground down the Viminal Hill and it is now hard to distinguish it from the adjoining Quirinal. As one of the Seven Hills, it once boasted a temple to Pan; nowadays, it has few monuments of which to be proud. Through its triumphal arch of an entrance ① the late 19thC **Palazzo delle Esposizioni** hosts important temporary art exhibitions in an impressively modern interior. ② **San Vitale**, another ancient church dressed in more modern garb, has a fine, if distressed, *trompe l'oeil* interior. ③ **Hotel Virgilio** (30, Via Palermo) is a peaceful stop in a convenient though none-too-inspiring part of the city (LL). The great 1920s mass of ④ **Palazzo del Viminale** houses the Ministero degli Interni. Amongst a string of restaurants in ⑤ Via del Boschetto are the basic **Frascati** (L) at No 28 with honest Roman cooking and **Bonne Nouvelle** (LL) at No 74 with seafood and class. ⑥ **Via Panisperna** runs like a roller-coaster over the Quirinal and Viminal hills. San Lorenzo – one of the city's most popular martyrs who once had some 30 Roman chapels to his name – traditionally met his grisly end in 258 on the site of ⑦ **San Lorenzo in Panisperna**. Stretched and burning on a gridiron, he is said to have called out, "The meat is done, make haste hither and eat". Little remains of the ancient foundations of the church.

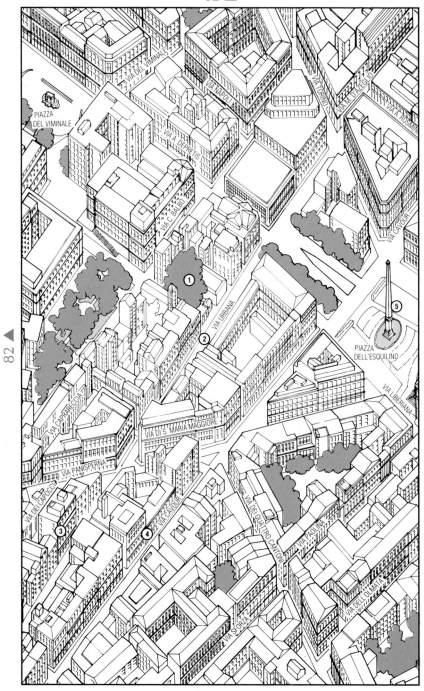

PIAZZA
DEL VIMINALE

VIA DEL VIMINALE

VIA NAPOLI

VIA TORINO

VIA M. D'AZEGLIO

VIA A. ROSMINI

VIA A. DEPRETIS

VIA C. BALBO

VIA URBANA

VIA CAVOUR

PIAZZA
DELL'ESQUILINO

VIA LIBERIANA

VIA CAPRAREDA

VIA DI S. MARIA MAGGIORE

VIA PANISPERNA

VIA DEI CAPOCCI

VIA CAVOUR

VIA DEL QUATTRO CANTONI

VIA PAOLINA

VIA SFORZA

VIA DELL'OLMATA

84

Via Cavour

Cutting a swath through Rome's history, the 19thC Via Cavour is lined with anonymous apartment blocks and rows of indifferent shops. On either side is a no-man's-land of glum backstreets that run between the Viminal Hill and Santa Maria Maggiore. The 1870's façade of ① **Santa Pudenziana** hardly suggests that this is one of the earliest churches in Rome, although its sunken position, well below the modern street level, is a clue to its ancient roots. Legend claims that St Peter stayed here in the house of one Senator Q. Cornelius Pudens, persuading the statesman and his two daughters, Pudenziana and Prassede, of the truth of Christianity. A chapel was first built over the spot in the reign of Pius I, some 100 years after Peter's death. In 384 it was rebuilt; the mosaics in the apse, reckoned amongst the earliest figurative representations surviving in any Roman church, date from this time. It is now the Philippine national church. ② Via Urbana has come down in the world; it was once the ancient Vicus Patricius, lined with the smart mansions of senators and patricians. Echoes of elegant living can still be found at ③ **Hosteria 104** (LL) at No 104, away from the traffic fumes in ④ **Via Cavour**. ⑤ The lonely **obelisk** that adorns Piazza dell'Esquilino once stood guard at the Mausoleum of Augustus; its twin is in Piazza Quirinale.

Santa Maria Maggiore

The villa and gardens of Montalto, once owned by the 16thC Pope Sixtus V, stretched from Piazza dell'Esquilino to where Termini Station now stands. In the building boom that followed the Unification of Italy in 1870, it was swept away along with much else of beauty. Happily one of Rome's finest churches still remains, tranquilly surveying the grimy 19thC *palazzi* and the sea of cars that surround it. Looming over Piazza dell'Esquilino, the twin-domed Baroque rump of ① **Santa Maria Maggiore** little prepares you for the ancient splendour inside one of the city's four great Patriarchal basilicas. The summit of the Esquiline Hill was once dedicated to the cult of the mother goddess Juno Lucina; it is perhaps no coincidence that Pope Sixtus III (432-40) built a basilica to the Mother of God on the same spot. The three naves are flanked by a stately procession of 40 marble and granite pillars pillaged from Classical ruins while glowing 5thC mosaics decorate the walls above. Even the ubiquitous Baroque monumental chapels are well tucked away in what is one of Rome's finest larger churches. ② Fuga's florid **façade** (1750) looks down on ③ the sole surviving **Corinthian column** from the ancient Basilica di Massenzio, brought here from the Forum in 1615 and topped with a bronze Madonna. A worn Romanesque portal (1269) sits uncomfortably in the 20thC façade of ④ the Russian church of **Sant'Antonio Abate**. ⑤ The friendly **Birreria Marconi** (10, Via di Santa Prassede) caters for Teutonic tastes (L). The small basilica of ⑥ **Santa Prassede** guards Rome's most important Byzantine monument. Built in 822 by Pope Pasqual I as a mausoleum for his mother Teodora, the **Cappella di San Zenone** is sheathed in lambent mosaics in gold and polychrome hues. Part of the column to which Christ was said to have been bound for the Flagellation stands in the chapel under a glass dome. Yet more dazzling mosaics decorate the arch and apse above the church's main altar. Pope Gregory XIII (1572-85) built ⑦ **Via Merulana** as a ceremonial way between Santa Maria Maggiore and its sister Basilica of St John Lateran (see page 125).

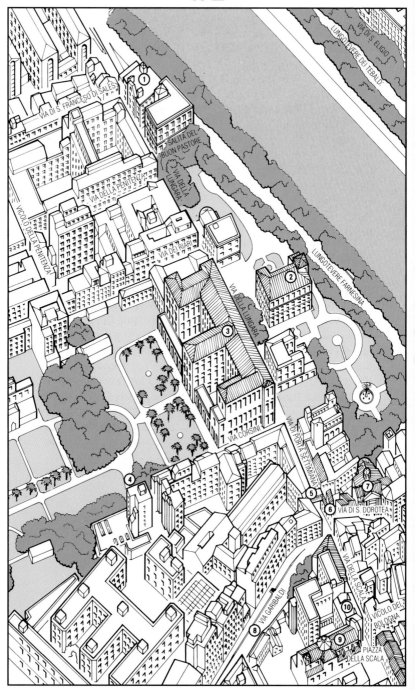

Palazzo Corsini and Villa Farnesina

The 19thC fortress façade of ① **Regina Coeli Prison** leaves little doubt as to the building's use. On the threshold of medieval Trastevere, the fabulously rich Sienese banker, Agostino Chigi, built ② **Villa Farnesina** (1511). Here he gave impressive dinners where the solid silver dishes and cutlery would be thrown into the Tiber after each course. Like any financier, however, he made sure he could recover his assets and arranged an underwater net to retrieve them after the feast. Raphael was responsible for the beautiful fresco cycle of *Cupid and Psyche* (1517) that decorates the loggia. Upstairs is Peruzzi's *Salone delle Prospettive*, a bewitching example of early Renaissance perspective trickery. Behind the ample façade of Ferdinando Fuga's ③ **Palazzo Corsini** (1736) is a noteworthy gallery of 16th and 17thC painting and the seat of the Accademia dei Lincei, the world's oldest scientific academy. The gardens of the palace are now Rome's **Botanic Gardens**, the Orto Botanico (entrance at ④), 12 hectares of restful lushness. A late 15thC castellated gateway, ⑤ the **Porta Settimiana**, stands on the site of a Roman postern gate that pierced the Aurelian Wall. An antique column in the wall and a delicate frieze around the upper window mark ⑥ the **house of Raphael's mistress**, La Fornarina, the Baker's Daughter (20, Via Santa Dorotea). Vasari narrates how the artist's work for Agostino Chigi suffered so much because of his infatuation that Chigi agreed to her living in the Farnesina while Raphael was working there. Next door at **Ristorante Romolo**, you can eat in her garden (LL). Around the corner, at ⑦ the church of Santa Dorotea, **Europe's first free school** was opened in 1597. ⑧ **Via Giuseppe Garibaldi** climbs the flanks of the Janiculum (off map). Rising to 85 m, its park affords sweeping views of the city. Next to ⑨ the 16thC church of **Santa Maria della Scala** is ⑩ the last surviving **monastic pharmacy** in Rome.

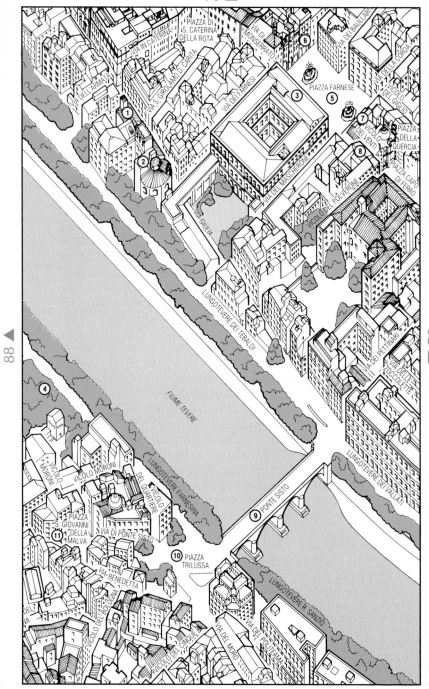

① Baroque **Palazzo Falconiere**, embellished with bizarre falcon-headed, bare-breasted torsos designed by Borromini, stands at the southern end of Via Giulia (see map page 68). Next door, macabre winged skulls decorate ② the church of **Santa Maria dell'Orazione e Morte**, rebuilt in 1737 and used by a confraternity dedicated to providing Christian burials for the unidentified dead. Alongside the church, the road is spanned by a creeper-clad bridge, the only realized part of a project to link ③ **Palazzo Farnese** with ④ **Villa Farnesina** across the Tiber (see page 89). Cardinal Alessandro Farnese (1468-1549), later Pope Paul III, was said in his day to possess Rome's three most beautiful treasures – his daughter, the church of Il Gesù and Palazzo Farnese. The monumental palace is the finest of Rome's 16thC *palazzi* and was begun in 1514 by Sangallo the Younger. The imposing upper storeys are the work of Michelangelo. It now houses the French Embassy in not only one of the world's finest ambassadorial buildings but also one of the cheapest – the current rent is one Lira every 99 years. The two colossal Egyptian granite bowls of Rainaldi's twin fountains for ⑤ **Piazza Farnese** were brought from the ruins of the Baths of Caracalla. The nuns in ⑥ **Santa Brigida** wear a characteristic Swedish wimple decorated with crossed azure tapes. The Swedish saint, remembered for her outspoken advice to the popes of her time, died in 1373 in the house next door. Across the piazza, French influences colour the menu at ⑦ up-market **Camponeschi** (50, Piazza Farnese), (LLL). The jaunty frontage of ⑧ **Palazzo Spada** (1540) is punctuated by statues of ancient Rome's great statesmen decked with lavish stucco festoons. The palace houses the **Galleria Spada**, a small but perfectly formed Seicento art collection, and Borromini's *trompe l'oeil* **Galleria Prospettica** – his ingenious trickery makes the gallery seem twice its length. The Consiglio di Stato, Italy's cabinet, is housed in the upper floor of the palace. Collapse seems imminent for ⑨ traffic-free **Ponte Sisto**, Rome's first Papal bridge, built in 1474 by Pope Sixtus IV on the site of Marcus Aurelius' Pons Aurelianus. Facing the bridge, ⑩ **Piazza Trilussa** has a fine fountain set high in a Baroque portico and a bronze of the eponymous Roman dialect poet (1871-1950). ⑪ **Piazza San Giovanni della Malva**, hemmed in by restaurants, bars, a church, and copious crumbling plaster, has the typical elements of Trastevere.

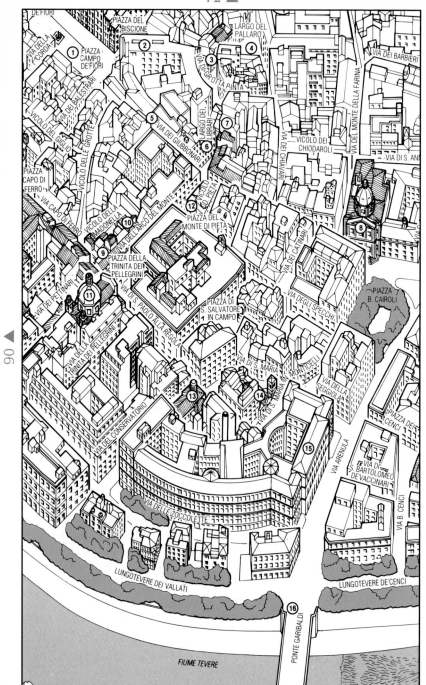

① **Piazza Campo de' Fiori** was once a stage for public executions. The Renaissance sceptic Giordano Bruno, whose hooded statue looms above the square, was burnt alive here in 1600 under orders of the Inquisition. Today, it is Rome's most vibrant food market with a small-town atmosphere and a host of alluring shops – look out for the bakery **Il Forno di Campo de' Fiori** at No 22, the pork butcher **Antica Norcineria Viola** at No 43 and the wine shop **Vineria Reggio** at No 15. ② The 17thC **Palazzo Pio** was built on the ruins of the vast **Teatro di Pompeo** (61-55 BC), ancient Rome's first permanent theatre which seated some 27,000 spectators – the curve of ③ Via di Grotta Pinta follows the line of its stage. A few paces to the east was the Senate Hall where Julius Caesar was murdered on the fateful ides of March, 44 BC. ④ The tiny, tastefully restored **Hotel Teatro di Pompeo** (8, Largo del Pallaro) is built into the remains of the theatre (LL). ⑤ **Via dei Giubbonari** – the street of the jacket-makers – is aptly lined with unpretentious clothes shops. ⑥ **Largo dei Librari** used to be the place for booksellers. ⑦ **Er Filettaro** (88, Largo dei Librari) is an historic fried food shop famed for its battered fillets of *baccalà*, salt cod – tables are hard to find (L). ⑧ San **Carlo ai Catinari** (1620), whose name recalls the chainmakers' workshops that once stood nearby, has a fine cupola and a chapel tricked out with false perspectives. Classical pillars and architraves are built into the walls of ⑨ **31, Via Capo di Ferro** – a fine example of medieval recycling of ancient remains. ⑩ **Il Pianeta Terra** (95, Via Arco del Monte) is widely hailed as one of the city's most epicurean and imaginative restaurants (LLL). ⑪ The church of **Trinità dei Pellegrini** and its adjoining hospice were built for pilgrims coming to Rome for the 1625 Jubilee – some 600,000 of them turned up on the doorstep. ⑫ **Palazzo del Monte di Pietà** once housed an institute for the poor; it is now used by a bank. St Paul is said to have passed two years of his imprisonment in Rome in a house that stood on the site of ⑬ **San Paolo alla Regola**. The crumbling Baroque façade of ⑭ **Santa Maria in Monticelli** pushes aside a fine Romanesque campanile. ⑮ The sprawling offices of the **Ministero di Grazia e Giustizia** (the Ministry of Grace and Justice) built 1913-32. ⑯ **Ponte Garibaldi** (1888) links the left bank of the Tiber with Trastevere.

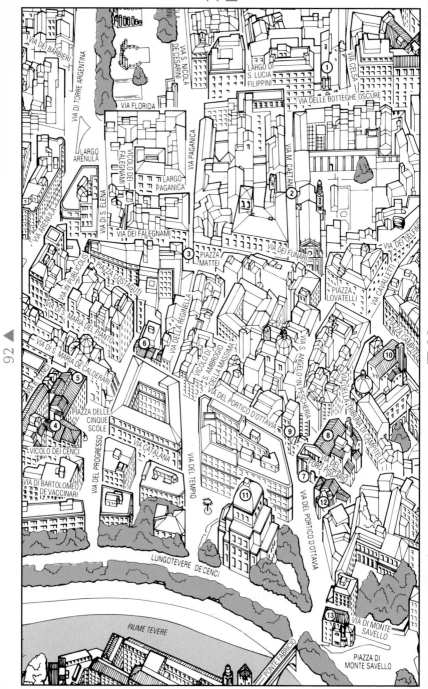

The Ghetto

Rome's Jewish community, one of the oldest in Europe, dates back to around 140 BC and was to be instrumental in first bringing Christianity to the city. Jews in Rome enjoyed relative security until 1555 when they were rounded up by Pope Paul IV and forced to live in the Ghetto. Its walls were finally pulled down in the late 19thC but some 5,000 Jews still live and work here. ① A pair of Corinthian columns and scattered fragments, the **ruins of an unidentified ancient temple**, were found during road widening in the 1930s. A **plaque** in ② Via Caetani marks the spot where the bullet-riddled body of ex-Prime Minister Aldo Moro was found on the morning of the 9th May, 1978. Rome's most beguiling late Renaissance fountain stands in ③ Piazza Mattei. The **Fontana delle Tartarughe**, designed by Giacomo della Porta (1584) and sculpted in bronze by Taddeo Landini, features four lithe youths holding aloft tortoises to drink from the upper bowl. ④ The sinister **palazzo of the tragic Cenci family**, an architectural mish-mash dating back to the 16thC, was built on the ruins of the great Circus Flaminius (221 BC). ⑤ **Al Pompiere** (discreet entrance at 38, Via Santa Maria dei Calderari) has some of the finest Roman Jewish cooking to be found in the Ghetto, in grand upstairs rooms of Palazzo Cenci (LL). 'Restored in the 2,221st year after the founding of Rome' (ie. 1497) reads the Latin tablet ⑥ at 1, Via del Portico di Ottavia. ⑦ **The Portico di Ottavia**, originally erected in 146 BC and rebuilt in 27-23 BC by Augustus, once encircled temples to Jupiter and Juno. Part of the ruins now forms the entrance to ⑧ **Sant'Angelo in Pescheria**, a church that recalls in its name the fish market that stood here until 1888. Pillars from the Portico flank the terrace of ⑨ **Da Giggetto**, a good place to try fried *carciofi* (artichokes) and *baccalà* (salt cod) (LL). In ⑩ **Santa Maria in Campitelli**, a fine church by Rainaldi (1667), a gilt 'sunburst' over the main altar frames one of Rome's many miraculous portraits of the Madonna. ⑪ Rome's synagogue is Belle Epoque with Babylonian strains; also note the aluminium-clad dome. Inside is the Jewish Museum. ⑫ A memorial records the Nazi round-up of Roman Jews – of the 2,091 sent to concentration camps, only 15 returned. Until the close of the 18thC, Jews were obliged to gather every Saturday at ⑬ **San Gregorio a Ponte Quattro Capi** to listen to sermons exhorting them to convert to Christianity.

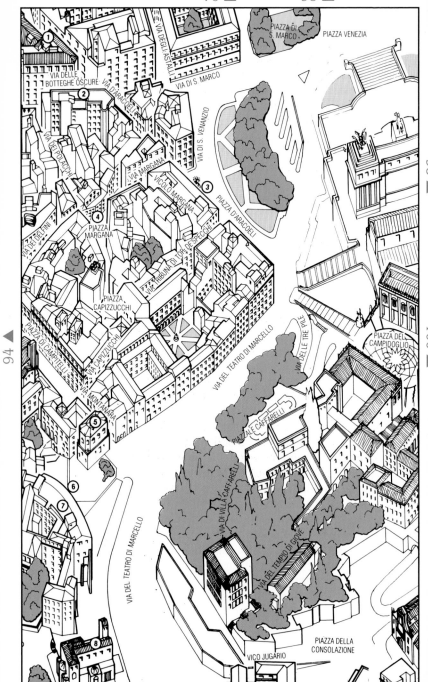

PIAZZA DI
S. MARCO   PIAZZA VENEZIA

VIA DEGLI ASTALLI

VIA DI S. MARCO

VIA DELLE
BOTTEGHE OSCURE

VIA D'ARACOELI

VIA DI S. VENANZIO

VIA MARGANA

VICOLO MARGANA

PIAZZA D'ARACOELI

VIA DEI DELFINI

VIA DEI POLACCHI

PIAZZA
MARGANA

VIA TRIBUNA DI TOR DE' SPECCHI

PIAZZA
CAPIZZUCCHI

VIA CAPIZZUCCHI

PIAZZA DI CAMPITELLI

VIA MONTANARA

VIA DEL TEATRO DI MARCELLO

VIA DELLE TRE PILE

PIAZZA DEL
CAMPIDOGLIO

PIAZZALE CAFFARELLI

VIA DI VILLA CAFFARELLI

VIA DEL TEMPIO DI GIOVE

VIA DEL TEATRO DI MARCELLO

PIAZZA DELLA
CONSOLAZIONE

VICO JUGARIO

An Aladdin's cave of braids and tassles at ① **Martino** (37, Via d' Aracoeli); next door, **Paganini** has a vast selection of fabrics to match. Il Partito Democratico della Sinistra, the former Italian Communist Party, has its headquarters in ② a reddish palazzo on **Via delle Botteghe Oscure**. Built into the arches of an ancient Roman theatre, the gloomy workshops, or *botteghe*, that gave the street its name have long since been swept away. Another of Giacomo della Porta's fountains – Rome would be much the poorer without his numerous watery works – decorates ③ **Piazza d'Aracoeli**; this time putti pour water from jugs into double- decker basins (1589). The square is overshadowed by the Capitoline Hill and and the bludgeoning bulk of the Monumento Nazionale (see map page 98). A few paces from the hubbub of Piazza Venezia, ④ **Piazza Margana** is a pleasant oasis. Of a summer's evening, **Trattoria Angelino**, No 37, has candle-lit tables in the square. ⑤ Carlo Fontana's biscuit-box Baroque church of **Santa Rita** (1665) was moved from the edge of the Capitoline Hill in 1940 and now stands primly beside the ruins of ⑥ the **Temple of Apollo Sosiano**. Built on the site of an earlier temple in 32 BC, three beautiful Corinthian columns are all that remain. Overshadowing it is the imposing ruin of ⑦ the **Theatre of Marcellus** (completed in 11 BC) whose great arches echo the Colosseum. Only in Rome could such a striking pile be topped by a fortress palace, in this case built by the powerful Orsini in the early 16thC. Until the Fascist clean-up of the area, the great theatre lay buried up to its ankles, its arches filled with half-derelict workshops. More ancient memories at ⑧ **San Nicola in Carcere**: the columns built into the flanks of the church were once part of a group of three Republican temples that stood in the midst of Ancient Rome's fruit and vegetable market, the Foro Olitorio. Antique rubble litters the surrounding lawns.

VIA DEI FORNARI

VICOLO DI S. BERNARDO

PIAZZA DELLA MADONNA DI LORETO

PIAZZA DI S. MARCO

PIAZZA VENEZIA

VIA DI S. MARCO

VIA DEI FORI IMPERIALI

PIAZZA D'ARACOELI

SCALA DELL'ARCE CAPITOLINA

VIA DI S. PIETRO IN CARCERE

VIA DEL TEATRO DI MARCELLO

VIA DELLE TRE PILE

PIAZZA DEL CAMPIDOGLIO

VIA DEL TULLIANO

PIAZZALE CAFFARELLI

VIA DEL CAMPIDOGLIO

VIA DI VILLA CAFFARELLI

VIA DEL TEMPIO DI GIOVE

VIA MONTE TARPEO

The Capitoline Hill

From the early days of the Etruscan kings, the smallest of Rome's seven hills was the sacred heart of the ancient city, crowned by the great temple to Jupiter Optimus Maximus. It was here that victorious generals came to give thanks to the father of the gods and that consuls swore their allegiance. At the base of the hill, ① the sturdy early Renaissance **Palazzo Venezia**, begun in 1451, was the seat of the Venetian Embassy. In the Fascist years, Mussolini used it as his headquarters; it now houses a museum with a fine collection of medieval art. A score of Venetian cardinals is buried in ② **San Marco**, an ancient church later incorporated into the palace. The glaring white marble ③ **Monumento Nazionale** (1885-1911), built to honour United Italy's first king, Vittorio Emanuele II, rises arrogantly above the Roman skyline, failing dismally to complement the Classical ruins below it. ④ The **Tomb of C. Publius Bibulus** was a noted landmark in Imperial times. ⑤ A steep flight of 122 **steps** climbs to ⑥ **Santa Maria d'Aracoeli**. The Romanesque Gothic church, built by the Franciscans in the 1300s on the foundations of an earlier church, stands on the highest point of the Capitoline Hill. Long before, it had been the site of the ancient Roman *arx*, or citadel, and the temple to Juno Moneta which also housed the Roman mint – her name lives on in 'moneta', or money. Michelangelo's broad ramp of ⑦ the **Cordonata**, topped by colossal antique statues of Castor and Pollux, leads up to his majestic *mise en scène* for ⑧ **Piazza del Campidoglio**. Michelangelo was also responsible for the basic design of the three palaces that flank it. ⑨ **Palazzo Nuovo** and ⑩ **Palazzo dei Conservatori** form the **Capitoline Museums,**• an outstanding hoard that includes a peerless assembly of Classical sculpture. The world's oldest public collection, it was founded in 1471 by Pope Sixtus IV. The gilded equestrian statue of Marcus Aurelius, until recent years the square's celebrated centrepiece, now shelters in the Palazzo Nuovo. It survived the centuries only because it was mistaken for the Christian Emperor Constantine. ⑪ **Palazzo del Senatore**, the official seat of the Commune of Rome, was built over the ruins of the *Tabularium*, the ancient records office dating from 78 BC. Traitors were thrown off the **Tarpeian Rock**, ⑫, named after the treacherous Tarpeia who betrayed the Romans to the Sabines in the founding days of the city.

PIAZZA
VENEZIA

VIA ALESSANDRINA

VIA DI S. PIETRO IN CARCERE

VIA DEL TULLIANO

VIA DEI FORI IMPERIALI

VIA DELLA SALARA VECCHIA

PIAZZA DEL
CAMPIDOGLIO

VIA DELLA CURIA

VIA DELLA
CONSOLAZIONE

VIA DE' FORAGGI

VIA DI S. TEODORO

① Mussolini's grandiose **Via dei Fori Imperiali** drove a wedge between the original Roman Forum and its later extensions, collectively known as the Imperial Forums. ② **Trajan's Forum** was the last and grandest of these additions while ③ the **Forum of Caesar** was the first. The rudimentary ruins convey little of their former majesty. Tradition has it that St Peter was imprisoned in the noisome dungeon beneath ④ **San Giuseppe dei Falegnami**. Probably built as a water cistern around 387 BC, it formed the lower vault of the grisly Mamertine prison. The **Roman Forum**, the city's great meeting place, grew up in the hollow between four of Rome's hills. Its celebrated ruins span some 1,000 years of construction, layer upon layer. Before wandering among the broken columns (entrance on Via dei Fori Imperiali – see ⑧ on page 102) survey the site from ⑤ or ⑥ on the flanks of the Capitoline Hill. Directly below, three fluted Corinthian columns topped by a fragment of architrave are all that remain of ⑦ the **Temple of Vespasian**, raised to his father by the tyrannical Domitian in AD 81. ⑧ The **Arch of Septimius Severus**, built for the Emperor's tenth anniversary, became the model for triumphal arches across the world. Mark Antony made his famous speech after Caesar's murder from the shattered platform of ⑨ the **Rostra**. Next to the incongruous 17thC church of ⑩ **San Luca** is ⑪ the **Curia**, the only intact building in the Forum, rebuilt several times during its history as the Senate House, converted into a church in the 7thC and finally stripped of its later Baroque trappings in the 1930s. Saturnalia, the pagan Christmas, was celebrated in ⑫ the **Temple of Saturn** – eight granite columns of its portico still stand. ⑬ The lone **Column of Phocas**, a late addition to the Forum, was erected in 608. ⑭ The vast **Basilica Giulia**, where the acclaimed lawyer Cicero addressed the crowded courts, is now reduced to its foundations. The same fate has befallen ⑮ the **Basilica Aemilia**, built in 179 BC as a business exchange and destroyed in Alaric's Sack of Rome in 410. ⑯ The **Temple of Julius Caesar** was erected on the spot where he was cremated. Six columns support the dedication on ⑰ the **Temple of Antoninus and Faustina**; a Baroque church peeps out from behind. Three of the Forum's finest Corinthian columns testify to the beauty of ⑱ the **Temple of Castor and Pollux**. The original rudimentary straw hut gave its form to ⑲ the later circular stone **Temple of Vesta**.

Piazza del Grillo is bordered by ① the medieval **Casa dei Cavalieri di Rodi**, the old priory of the Knights of Malta. Behind it lie the curved walls of ② the **Forum of Augustus** that frame the ruins of ③ the **Temple of Mars Ultor** – Mars the Avenger – completed in 2 BC to keep alive the memory of the murder of Julius Caesar. Little can now be seen of ④ the adjacent **Forum of Nerva**, much of which now lies under modern roads. Petrarch considered the formidable 13thC **Torre dei Conti**, ⑤, built as a papal watchtower, one of the wonders of Rome. The severed stump that remains is still impressive. ⑥ The plush **Hotel Forum** (25, Via Tor de' Conti) has glorious views over the Forum (LLL). ⑦ Next door is one of Rome's more recherché museums, the **Museo del Presepio**, or Christmas cribs (open Wed and Sat 6 pm to 8 pm, Oct to May). ⑧ The **main entrance** to the ruins of both the Roman Forum and the Palatine Hill (see pages 119 and 121) is off the Via dei Fori Imperiali (open Wed to Sat and Mon 9 am-6 pm; until 3 pm in winter; Sun and Tues until 1 pm). The early church of ⑨ **Santi Cosmo e Damiano** (enter from outside the Forum) was built in a hall of Vespasian's Forum of Peace. The original bronze doors of ⑩ the 4thC **Temple of Romulus**, dedicated to usurping Emperor Maxentius' son rather than the city's legendary founder, serve as the church's rear entrance. Traversing the Forum, the ancient ceremonial way ⑪ of the **Sacra Via** witnessed the triumphal processions of Rome's returning generals. The three 24-m high arches of ⑫ the **Basilica of Maxentius**, begun around 310 and one of the last great monuments to Classical architecture, still dwarf the rest of the Forum. The concrete vaulting provided the inspiration for many a Renaissance building. Around the primitive Temple of Vesta (see page 101) rose ⑬ the **House of the Vestal Virgins**, the famed priestesses who tended Rome's Sacred Flame. Although they lived in pampered state, a fall from virginity during their 30-year office meant burial alive. ⑭ The church of **Santa Francesca Romana**, crowned by its splendid Romanesque campanile, guards the remains of the patron saint of Roman drivers. On her Feast Day, March 9, cars fill the main road to be blessed (entrance from Via dei Fori Imperiali). The monastery behind the church is now ⑮ the **Antiquarium Forense**, a dingy museum housing finds from the archaic necropoli that pre-date the Forum (entrance within the Forum).

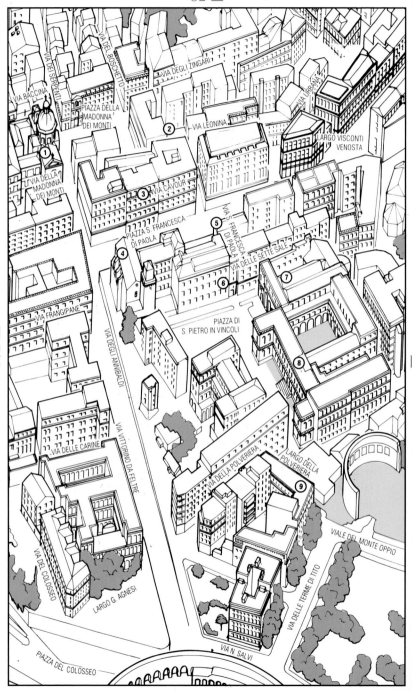

VIA BACCINA

VIA DEI SERPENTI

VIA DEL BOSCHETTO

VIA DEGLI ZINGARI

VIA URBANA

PIAZZA DELLA MADONNA DEI MONTI

VIA LEONINA

① ② ③ ④ ⑤ ⑥ ⑦ ⑧ ⑨

LARGO VISCONTI VENOSTA

VIA DELLA MADONNA DEI MONTI

VIA CAVOUR

PIAZZA S. FRANCESCA DI PAOLA

VIA S. FRANCESCA DI PAOLA

VIA DELLE SETTE SALE

VIA FRANGIPANE

VIA DEGLI ANNIBALDI

PIAZZA DI S. PIETRO IN VINCOLI

VIA VITTORINO DA FELTRE

VIA DELLE CARINE

VIA DELLA POLVERIERA

LARGO DELLA POLVERIERA

VIALE DEL MONTE OPPIO

VIA DEL COLOSSEO

LARGO G. AGNESI

VIA DELLE TERME DI TITO

PIAZZA DEL COLOSSEO

VIA N. SALVI

San Pietro in Vincoli

Giacomo della Porta's self-assured church of ① **Madonna dei Monti** (1580) has an artful High Baroque interior. ② The small and tastefully restored **Hotel Duca d'Alba** (14, Via Leonina) stands in a peaceful backwater (LL). Imposing ramparts that buttress the flanks of the Esquiline Hill mark the western end of ③ the congested **Via Cavour**. ④ **San Francesco di Paola**, now no longer used by the austere Minim Friars, is sadly dilapidated. ⑤ The steps of ⑤ **Via San Francesco di Paola** follow the course of the ancient Vicus Sceleratus, Accursed Street. Tullia, the ambitious daughter of Rome's penultimate king, Servius Tullius, paved her husband's way to the throne by arranging her father's death. Adding profanity to murder, she drove her chariot over his corpse, splattering her dress with his blood. The ghosts of more recent monsters haunt ⑥ the 16thC **Case Borgia** – distinctive black-and-white striped stonework peeps through the rendering. On the crest of the hill stands ⑦ **San Pietro in Vincoli**, St Peter in Chains, an ancient church with two attractions that draw the curious by the coachload: the chains said to have bound St Peter, and Michelangelo's celebrated statue of Moses. The iron fetters, preserved in a glass casket below the main altar, were reputedly brought from Jerusalem in the 5thC. Michelangelo's powerful Old Testament vision of Moses is the centrepiece to the Tomb of Pope Julius II. The mausoleum was to have been the highlight of St Peter's Basilica, complete with some 40 other figures, but endless argument with Julius and his successors meant it was never finished; the mighty prophet is reduced to consorting with much inferior statues by Michelangelo's pupils. Fine monochrome 19thC frescoes dedicated to the scientific arts decorate the warm stone of ⑧ **Rome University's Faculty of Engineering**. ⑨ Where Nero's Golden House once stood, **Da Nerone** (96, Via delle Terme di Tito) is a pleasant restaurant that has not suffered from its proximity to the Colosseum (LL).

Nero's Golden House and The Baths of Trajan

Two messed-about **towers** ① and ② are all that remain of the stronghold of the once-powerful medieval Cappoci family. Modern parkland dotted with hefty chunks of Roman masonry (see ④ below) now covers the slopes of Colle Oppio, an outlying peak of the city's seven hills. Nero, whose conceit even nurtured a plan to rename Rome Neropolis, built his legendary Domus Aurea, or Golden House, here, on the ruins of the Roman suburb laid waste by the great fire of AD 64 (when he is reputed to have fiddled while Rome burnt). The fabulous palace, however, proved too concrete a reminder of the Emperor's excesses and was razed around AD 100 to make way for Trajan's magnificent Baths. The **remnants** of ③ the **Domus Aurea** (set for a lengthy closure for repairs) lie underground beside the south-western entrance to the park. The approach to this *folie de grandeur* was marked by a colossal 35-m gilded bronze statue of the Emperor; inside, walls were gilded and studded with precious stones and mother-of-pearl while the dining rooms had ceilings of fretted ivory which slid back to rain flowers or perfumes upon his guests. Raphael was one of the artists much influenced by the delicate frescoes when rooms of the buried palace were unearthed in Renaissance times. ④ The lofty, precarious walls that punctuate the park are the **vestiges of Trajan's Baths** that obliterated Nero's pleasure palace. This monumental complex provided the model for the later, more celebrated, baths of Caracalla and Diocletian, but the ruins now give little idea of the building's grandeur.

The Esquiline Hill

A mournful air hangs over the modern parks and streets of the Esquiline Hill, perhaps an atavistic echo of the vast necropolis that once covered the area. Or maybe the ghost of Nero still haunts the place: his great Domus Aurea (see page 107) once stretched as far as here. The sturdy tufa blocks along the right-hand flank of ① **San Martino ai Monti** date back to Republican times. Inside, the broad nave carried by Corinthian columns – a ground-plan borrowed from the Classical Roman basilica from which most early churches developed – bears witness to the church's antiquity. The monolithic pile of ② **Palazzo Brancaccio** (1896) on busy Via Merulana houses the **Museo Nazionale d'Arte Orientale**, Italy's most important collection of Oriental art. Across the street, in a little island of greenery, is the entrance to ③ the **Auditorium di Mecenate** dating back to around 30 BC. Fragments of worn frescoed garden scenes still decorate what was probably once a grotto in the celebrated gardens of the Villa di Mecenate. ④ **Trattoria da Antonio** (19, Via Mecenate) – a cool retreat from the summer heat (L). ⑤ A fine gateway leads into the Parco Oppio (see page 107). ⑥ The **Sette Sale**, seven large tanks, supplied the water for Trajan's massive Baths (see page 107).

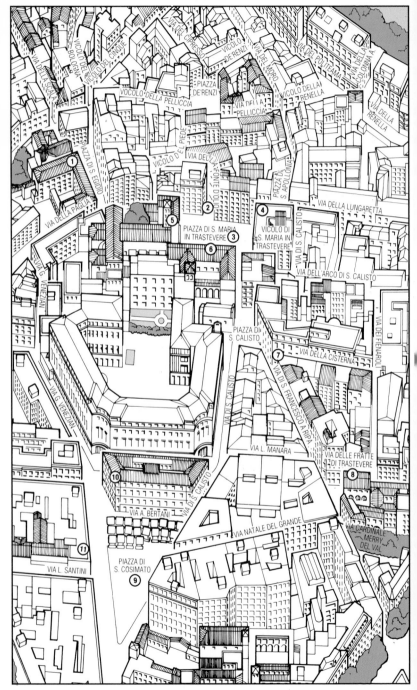

Santa Maria in Trastevere

The ancient plebeian district *(rione)* of Trastevere: Trastevere means 'across the Tiber' (Il Tevere) – it lies on the opposite bank of the river to the rest of the ancient city. The area claims to be the guardian of true Romanità, popular traditional culture that traces its roots back to Classical times. Despite growing gentrification, it still displays plenty of romantic neglect and offers entertaining night life. ① The **Museo del Folklore**, next door to the scrubbed Baroque church of Sant'Egidio, conjures up the spirits of earlier centuries in Rome. ② **Via della Fonte d'Olio** recalls the miraculous fount of oil that sprang from the earth here shortly before the birth of Christ. ③ **Piazza di Santa Maria in Trastevere** is the traffic-free heart of the district, pulsing with vitality of a summer's evening. ④ **Sabatini** at No 13 (LLL) is the smartest place from which to watch it. The façade of ⑤ **Santa Maria in Trastevere**, the earliest church in the city dedicated to the cult of the Virgin, is faced with glowing mosaics. Founded in the 3rdC, it was rebuilt around 1140. Despite subsequent restorations, it has retained much of its antique glory, including the outstanding mosaics over the apse. To the south of the square stands the blank face of ⑥ **Palazzo di San Callisto**, occupied by Vatican offices. On the corner of Via della Cisterna, ⑦ an inviting drinking fountain has a barrel and two wine flasks spouting water. ⑧ **San Pasquale Baylon**, built in 1122 but much knocked about in the 18thC, is Rome's church for *zitelle*, spinsters who come here to pray for the elusive Signor Right. ⑨ **Piazza San Cosimato**, a busy work-a-day centre, has a pair of exceptional fish restaurants, ⑩ **Alberto Ciarla** at No 40 – celebrated and luxurious (LLL); – and ⑪ **Corsetti Il Galeone** (LL) at No 27. The streets around also boast a score of no-nonsense, cheap Trastevere *pizzerie*, most with wood ovens and a warm welcome.

110 ◄

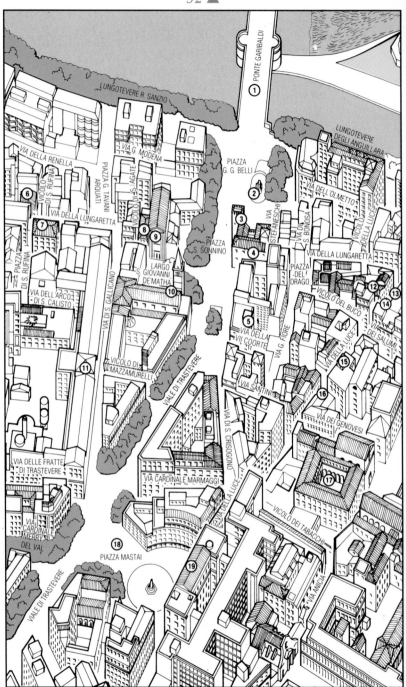

In the early days of Imperial Rome, Trastevere's cosmopolitan population included sailors who worked the great awnings of the Colosseum, skilled as they were at handling large areas of canvas. The city's Hebrew community also lived here and through them Christianity first arrived in Rome. The neighbourhood's pride in its ancient roots has kept alive a strong sense of popular tradition and a sturdy, if incomprehensible dialect. At the southern end of ① **Ponte Garibaldi** stands ② a statue to one of its greatest sons, the 19thC Roman dialect poet Gioachino Belli. The eclectic medieval ③ **Torre degli Anguillara** looms over the nearby Piazza Sidney Sonnino. It houses the Casa di Dante, not the great poet's house but an institute dedicated to his memory. The eastern end of ④ **Via della Lungaretta**, a street dating back to Classical times, still has the feel of old-time Trastevere. ⑤ The ruins of an Imperial Roman police-cum-fire station, occupied by the VII Coorte dei Vigili, were unearthed here in 1866. In the shadow of ⑥ the noble Romanesque campanile of **Sante Rufina e Seconda** is ⑦ **Da Cencia**, a small fish restaurant with pretty outdoor tables (LL). Jostling uncomfortably with ⑧ an Evangelical Baptist Church, the 18thC façade of ⑨ **Sant' Agata** looks across to one of Rome's more ancient churches, ⑩ **San Crisogono**. Rebuilt in 1129 on 5thC foundations, its worn antique columns and a luminous ceiling provide a haunting interior. Behind the long, low 18thC frontage of ⑪ the **Ospedale di San Gallicano** is a modern hospital. Opposite ⑫ **Santa Maria della Luce**, an ancient church with an 18thC refit, the art of Roman stucco work is kept alive in ⑬ the **workshops of the Baiocco family**. Next door, the luxurious ⑭ **Tentativo di Descrizione di un Banchetto a Roma** (5, Via della Luce) has a menu as mannered as its name (LLL). The name translates as 'attempt at a description of a banquet at Rome'. ⑮ Further down the street, at **No 21**, every type of biscuit imaginable is for sale, while ⑯ **Da Carlone**, No 27, has a happy mix of honest cooking at low prices (L). Rome's finest 15thC cloister lies hidden within the hospice of ⑰ **San Giovanni dei Genovesi**, built to care for the Genoese sailors disembarking at the nearby port of Ripa Grande (to view, ring at the entrance in Via Anicia between 3 and 5 pm). ⑱ **Piazza Mastai** on hectic Viale di Trastevere is watched over by ⑲ Pius IX's Neoclassical **officinam nicotianis foliis** or papal tobacco manufactory (1863), now the headquarters for Italy's state tobacco monopoly.

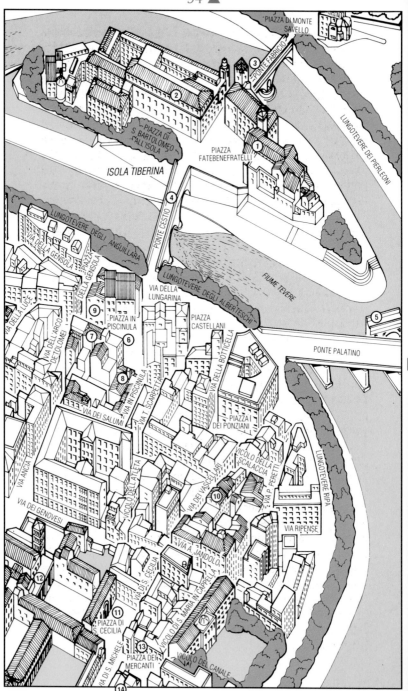

PIAZZA DI MONTE SAVELLO

PONTE FABRICIO

③

②

①

PIAZZA DI S. BARTOLOMEO ALL'ISOLA

PIAZZA FATEBENEFRATELLI

LUNGOTEVERE DEI PIERLEONI

ISOLA TIBERINA

④

PONTE CESTIO

LUNGOTEVERE DEGLI ANGUILLARA

VIA DELLA GENSOLA

PIAZZA DELLA GENSOLA

VIA DELLA LUCE

VIA DELL'ARCO DE' TOLOMEI

⑨ PIAZZA IN PISCINULA

⑦

⑥

⑧

VIA DELLA LUNGARINA

PIAZZA CASTELLANI

LUNGOTEVERE DEGLI ALBERTESCHI

FIUME TEVERE

⑤

PONTE PALATINO

VIA IN PISCINULA

VIA T. SCARPETTA

VIA DELLA BOTTICELLA

VIA DEI SALUMI

PIAZZA DEI PONZIANI

VIA ANICIA

VICOLO DELL'ATLETA

VIA DEI VASCELLARI

VICOLO DELLA SCALACCIA

VIA P. PERETTI

LUNGOTEVERE RIPA

⑩

VIA DEI GENOVESI

VIA RIPENSE

VIA A. JANDOLO

⑫

VIA DI S. CECILIA

VICOLO DI S. MARIA IN CAPPELLA

⑪ PIAZZA DI S. CECILIA

⑬ PIAZZA DEI MERCANTI

VICOLO DEL CANALE

VIA DI S. MICHELE

⑭ ▼

Fanciful legends surround the origins of the Isola Tiberina. Some believed that a boat sank here to form the 300 m-long island; others claimed that mud silted up around the Tarquins' hoard of grain, flung into the river by the people as they chased the last kings of Rome into exile. The island later became identified with the cult of Aesculapius, the god of medicine, to whom a temple was dedicated in 289 BC – the church of ① **San Bartolomeo** now stands in its place. The healing arts are still practised in ② the **Ospedale di San Giovanni di Dio** (founded 1548) by the Fatebenefratelli, which translates as the do-good brothers. Two of Rome's oldest bridges connect this curative haven to the mainland: one is ③ **Ponte Fabricio** to the north – also known as Quattro Capi from the eroded pair of four-headed herms that flank it – which dates from 62 BC; the other ④ is **Ponte Cestio**, erected in 46 BC. ⑤ A lonely arch standing in mid-stream is all that remains of **Ponte Rotto**, a 16thC reconstruction of the 2ndC BC Pons Aemilius. Away from the din of the Lungotevere, ⑥ **Piazza in Piscinula** has a typical Trastevere mix of smart restaurants, medieval *palazzi* and a sprinkling of antique fragments. ⑦ **Comparone**, No 47, provides an animated night out (LL). Above ⑧ **San Benedetto in Piscinula** sits a diminutive Romanesque campanile. To the north of the square stands ⑨ the crumbling medieval **Casa dei Mattei**. ⑩ **Da Enzo** (29, Via dei Vascellari) has unvarnished authenticity and proper food (L). A Late Baroque archway (1725) leads from ⑪ **Piazza Santa Cecilia** to the inviting courtyard of ⑫ **Santa Cecilia in Trastevere**, the shrine to the patron saint of music, shrouded in a cloth. Below the recently restored pastel interior, a maze of gloomy passages, the remains of an ancient building dating from Republican times and said to have been the martyr's home, leads to the richly decorated crypt where Santa Cecilia and her husband, San Valeriano, rest. ⑬ **Piazza Mercanti**, another of Trastevere's more colourful squares, is trying hard to resist the general sprucing-up of the neighbourhood. Like their predecessors the caesars, the popes kept the *populus* sweet with generous welfare provisions. The vast ⑭ **Ospizio di San Michele** (off map), founded by Innocent XII in 1693, provided a school, orphanage and old people's home – later, a borstal and a prison for women were added. Part of the building is being used as a temporary home for the celebrated collection of paintings from Villa Borghese, currently undergoing lengthy repairs.

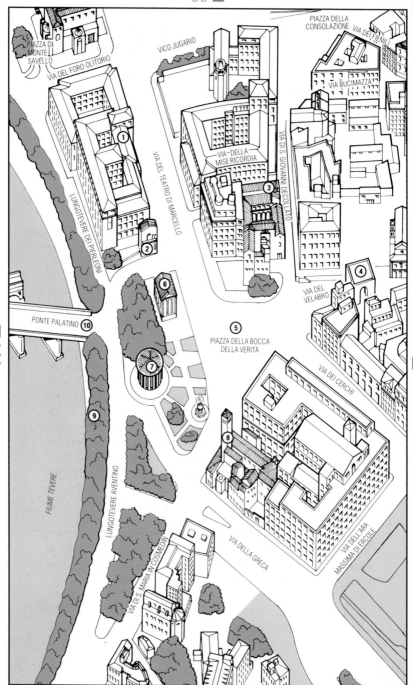

PIAZZA DELLA
CONSOLAZIONE — VIA DEI FIENILI

PIAZZA DI
MONTE
SAVELLO

VIA DEL FORO OLITORIO

VICO JUGARIO

VIA BUCIMAZZA

VIA DELLA
MISERICORDIA

VIA DEL TEATRO DI MARCELLO

VIA DI S. GIOVANNI DECOLLATO

LUNGOTEVERE DEI PIERLEONI

VIA DEL
VELABRO

PONTE PALATINO ⑩

PIAZZA DELLA BOCCA
DELLA VERITA

⑤

VIA DEI CERCHI

⑨

FIUME TEVERE

LUNGOTEVERE AVENTINO

VIA DI S. MARIA IN COSMEDIN

VIA DELLA GRECA

VIA DELL'ARA
MASSIMA DI ERCOLE

Facing one of Mussolini's grandiose thoroughfares, next to ①
the unendearing modern **Anagrafa**, or public records office, nes-
tles ② the **Casa dei Crescenzi**. Rich in plunder from Roman ruins,
it was built around 1100 by Rome's then most powerful family,
probably as a watchtower guarding the Tiber. Popular tradition
once claimed that it was Pontius Pilate's Roman *pied-à-terre*. ③
San Giovanni Decollato was completed in 1552 for a Florentine
confraternity – Michelangelo was a member – dedicated to eas-
ing the last hours of the condemned. Once a year, on June 24, a
grisly museum opens its doors to display such things as a regis-
ter of the executed and baskets which caught their heads. The
marble cube-shaped ④ **Arco di Giano**, or Arch of Janus, dates
from the reign of Constantine and marked the crossroads join-
ing the Roman Forum to some of the city's most important mar-
kets. The Forum Boarium, the ancient livestock market, stood
roughly on the site of ⑤ **Piazza Bocca della Verità** where a pair
of remarkably intact Republican temples still stand – to the north
⑥ the **Temple of Fortuna Virilis** and to the south ⑦ the circular
Temple of Vesta, the oldest marble temple in Rome. Both are
reckoned to be incorrectly named: the former was more likely
dedicated to the river god Portunus and the latter to Hercules
Victor. Despite its outstanding Romanesque campanile and
beguiling interior, tourists are drawn to the Greek church of ⑧
Santa Maria in Cosmedin to see the Bocca della Verità, the Mouth
of Truth. Worn and grimy from the grubby hands of centuries of
visitors, this Roman sewer cover in the form of a grotesque mask
shelters in the church's porchway. Celebrated as a medieval lie-
detector, it reputedly severed the fingers of those who spoke
falsely with their hands in its mouth. An English traveller was
reported to have had his scepticism shaken when his hand was
bitten by a scorpion while telling a tale. The city's largest sewer,
the **Cloaca Maxima**, was started in the reign of the Tarquins in
the 6thC BC. This exceptional, if unromantic, monument to early
Roman engineering was built to drain the marshy lands where
the Forum later grew up. At ⑨ is the arch of its opening, 5 m in
diameter, dating from the 2ndC BC and still feeding into the
Tiber just below ⑩ **Ponte Palatino**.

VIA DI S. TEODORO

VIA DEL VELABRO

VIA DEI CERCHI

The rise and fall of Classical Rome is written in the stones of the Palatine Hill – from Romulus and Remus to the bloated palaces of its emperors. ① The circular church of **San Teodoro**, which predates the 6thC, took root in the ruins of the *horrea* – the imperial storehouses which stood between the Forum and the Tiber. ② The **Domus Tiberiana** was the first of the grandiose imperial palaces which lorded it over the Palatine. Much of it was obliterated to make way for ③ the **Orti Farnesiani**, one of 16thC Europe's earliest and most exotic botanical gardens, designed by Vignola for the future Farnese Pope Paul III. Only a few walls remain of ④ the **palace** built by Tiberius' 24-year-old successor, the crazed Caligula. ⑤ A **belvedere** at the corner of the gardens takes in the whole history of Rome: beneath the railings, excavations of Iron Age Rome proceed around the legendary site of ⑥ the **Lupercal**, the cave where the wolf is said to have nurtured Rome's founder Romulus and his twin brother Remus; while ahead, the panorama encompasses St Peter's, the Capitoline Hill and the Monumento Nazionale. ⑦ Worn frescoes still decorate rooms leading off a sunken courtyard: known as the **House of Livia**, the wife of Augustus, it is now thought to have been an outbuilding of ⑧ Augustus's fine villa which stood nearby. ⑨ A stuccoed underground tunnel, the **Cryptoporticus**, leads to Domitian's ⑩ **Domus Flavia**, the Emperor's official palace. ⑪ **The Antiquarium**, housed in a 16thC villa, conserves wall paintings and sculptures found during excavations. Alongside the refreshingly primitive 6thC church of ⑫ **San Giorgio in Velabro** leans the **Arco degli Argentari**, erected in 204 in honour of Septimius Severus and his sons Caracalla and Geta – Caracalla had his brother's name and image erased after he had murdered him in 211. The bland façade of ⑬ **Sant'Anastasia** and its rich 17thC interior belie its ancient origins as the late Imperial parish church, once third in the hierarchy of Rome's churches. ⑭ The long, open arena of the **Circus Maximus** stands sadly abandoned at the side of one of Rome's traffic- clogged arteries. Built on the legendary site of the rape of the Sabine women, Rome's greatest race course could hold up to 300,000 spectators. The *spina*, or central island of the stadium, can still be clearly seen.

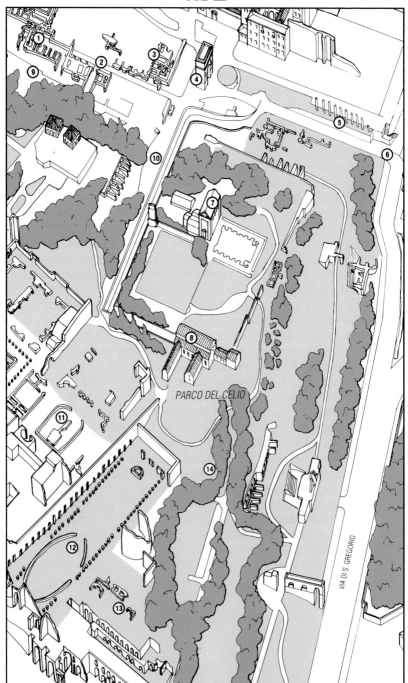

PARCO DEL CELIO

VIA DI S. GREGORIO

Grand Imperial palaces, each built to eclipse the others, have left the Palatine Hill a honeycomb of ruins that are hard to unravel. At the foot of the hill in the Roman Forum (see pages 101 and 103) behind ① the **House of the Vestal Virgins** lay ② **Via Nova**, an easily identifiable landmark among the ruins of the Forum, and ③ ruins of buildings thought to have formed part of the vestibule to Nero's Golden Palace and later used as warehouses. ④ The **Arch of Titus**, built in AD 81 to celebrate the destruction of Jerusalem, stands proudly above the Forum on the Velia, the spur which joined the Palatine to the Esquiline Hill. ⑤ Ten shattered columns mark the vast back-to-back temples, the largest in Rome, dedicated by Hadrian in 135 to Venus and Rome. Below them, ⑥ an **exit** from the Forum leads to the Colosseum. By the side of a ruined temple, the 10thC chapel of ⑦ **San Sebastiano**, set in a flowery garden, marks the spot where the soldier saint is said to have been shot through with arrows. Further along the track, ⑧ is the 17thC church of **San Bonaventura**. From ⑨ the **belvedere** of his palace, Tiberius could survey the Forum down below. ⑩ The rising path of **Clivus Palatinus** leads to ⑪ the vast **Domus Augustana** which was completed by Emperor Domitian in AD 96, a work which levelled a large chunk of the hill. This great colonnaded private palace adjoined the Emperor's official residence, the Domus Flavia, and reared up to dwarf even the great race track of the Circus Maximus below. The contemporary poet Statius described it as rising 'to kindle the jealousy of Jove himself'. Little now survives, except for several subterranean courtyards and a maze of underground rooms and passages too precarious to be open to public gaze. To the side lie the clearly discernible sunken remains of ⑫ **Domitian's stadium**. ⑬ The ruins of the **Domus Severiana**, the palace built for Emperor Septimius Severus at the end of the 2ndC, are among the best preserved of the Palatine buildings, but again they are too unsafe to be open to the public. From ⑭ the nearby **viewing point**, you get one of Rome's quintessential vistas over pines to the Colosseum.

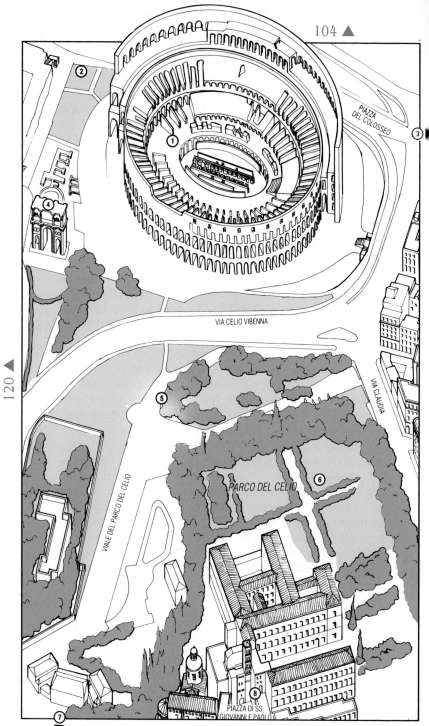

PIAZZA
DEL COLOSSEO

VIA CELIO VIBENNA

VIA CLAUDIA

VIALE DEL PARCO DEL CELIO

PARCO DEL CELIO

PIAZZA DI SS.
GIOVANNI E PAOLO

The Colosseum

There was an often-repeated prophecy that 'while stands the Colosseum, Rome shall stand; when falls the Colosseum, Rome shall fall; and when Rome falls, the world'. Despite earthquakes and plundering (to get materials for some of the city's finest Renaissance palaces) ① the **Colosseum** is still ancient Rome's greatest surviving glory. Inaugurated under the name of the Flavian Amphitheatre in AD 80 by Emperor Titus, the scale and barbarity of its spectacles soon became legendary – Suetonius describes one day alone when some 5,000 exotic wild beasts were killed. The 50,000 spectators, seated strictly according to their status, were shaded by huge canvas awnings and the great ring could be transformed into a lake for sea battles or a forest for hunts. From medieval times, the place was notorious for its beggars; today it is still the haunt of the city's unsavoury characters who prey on unwary tourists. The name Colosseum may have derived from Nero's colossal statue which stood nearby. Today a stone plaque ② marks its site. Wild cats now fight it out in the ruins of ③ the **Ludus Magnus** (off map), a miniature Colosseum that was once the main barracks and training ground for gladiators. The largest and best preserved of Rome's triumphal arches, ④ the **Arch of Constantine** was dedicated to the Emperor in 315 after his victory over the usurping Emperor Maxentius at Ponte Milvio. Note the phrase *instinctu divinitatis* ('by the will of the divinity') on the dedication above the main arch – the first, though veiled, official reference on the face of Imperial Rome to the newly adopted Christian God. Marooned by a matrix of major roads and tramways, ⑤ **Monte Celio**, once one of the most aristocratic of the seven hills, is strangely deserted. Much of the inhospitable parkland that covers it is becoming Rome's 'cardboard city'. Even the rudimentary remains of ⑥ the **Temple of Claudius**, later grabbed by Nero to form a *ninfeo*, or grotto, in the gardens of his Golden House (see page 107), are closed off. ⑦ The serene church of **San Gregorio Magno** (off map), on the southern flank of the hill, was built on the site of Gregory the Great's monastery where St Augustine took his leave before his journey to take Christianity to England. A medley of architectural styles surrounds ⑧ the small **Piazza Santi Giovanni e Paolo** ranging from the fine 12thC Romanesque campanile of the church to the Baroque gateway opposite.

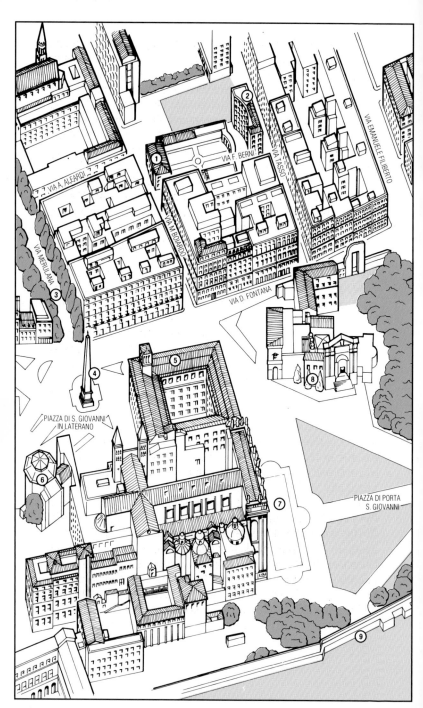

VIA EMANUELE FILIBERTO

VIA A. ALEARDI

VIA F. BERNI

VIA A. TASSO

VIA M. BOIARDO

VIA MERULANA

VIA D. FONTANA

PIAZZA DI S. GIOVANNI
IN LATERANO

PIAZZA DI PORTA
S. GIOVANNI

① The **Casino of Villa Giustiniani-Massimo** (open Tues, Thur and Sun) is decorated with frescoes by the Nazarenes, an early 19thC group of German painters intent on regenerating religious art. The English Pre-Raphaelite Movement were later to embrace their ideas. Behind the plain front of ② **145, Via Tasso**, the Nazi SS set up a notorious political prison in 1943. It now houses a museum commemorating the struggle for the liberation of Rome. The great processional way of ③ **Via Merulana** was laid out in the 16thC by Gregory XIII to link Santa Maria Maggiore with St John Lateran. ④ Rome's tallest and oldest Egyptian **obelisk** – 31 m of red granite some 3,500 years old and brought from Thebes in 357 – provides the centre-piece for Piazza San Giovanni in Laterano. ⑤ The **Lateran Palace** was the seat of the Papacy from the time of Constantine until it decamped to Avignon in 1305. Today's building (1586) was erected by Domenico Fontana as a summer palace for Sixtus V. Tucked away in a corner, ⑥ the octagonal **Baptistry** is the oldest building in the Lateran complex, erected by Sixtus III (432-40) over Constantine's original edifice – the Emperor is said to have been baptised in its basalt basin. A chorus line of titanic statues look down on the swirling traffic from Galilei's mighty 18thC façade of ⑦ **San Giovanni in Laterano**, the Cathedral of Rome and the mother of all Catholic churches. Scratch below Borromini's surprisingly restrained Baroque overhaul, completed in 1650, and there is plenty of evidence of the basilica's ancient roots. Founded in the 4thC on land given by Constantine, it was repeatedly destroyed and restored. The apse mosaics date from the 13thC while the soaring Gothic canopy over the papal altar was erected in 1367. Outstanding *Cosmati* work, the medieval Roman craft of inlaid marble, decorates the 13thC cloisters to the left of the church. ⑧ The **Scala Santa**, 28 marble steps that Christ is said to have climbed at his trial, is still traditionally ascended on bended knees. Martin Luther only got half way before standing up and walking back down. At the top is the **Sancta Sanctorum**, the ancient private chapel (firmly closed) of the popes that houses the Acheiropoeton ('not painted by human hand'), a celebrated early image of Christ once believed to have been the work of angels. 'There is no holier place in all the world', reads the inscription outside. ⑨ One of the best-preserved stretches of the **Aurelian Walls**, built by Marcus Aurelius between 271 and 275, which extended for 19 km and featured nearly 400 towers.

INDEX OF GENERAL POINTS OF INTEREST

INDEX OF PEOPLE OF INTEREST

INDEX OF PEOPLE OF INTEREST

INDEX OF STREET NAMES